This is the most impacting book Lee Grady has ever written. It has been exciting to watch Lee become a full-fledged disciple maker, like Jesus. *Follow Me* is not about theory—it's about lifestyle. Lee's journey is real, hands-on, heart given, time invested, and emotions exposed. This book is about how to reproduce Christ's life in others. You will never again question, "Should I make disciples?" I challenge you to read and then live this book. It is a game changer for the global church.

—NAOMI DOWDY
FORMER SENIOR PASTOR, APOSTOLIC LEADER,
TRINITY CHRISTIAN CENTRE
SINGAPORE

This book is a gift to this generation. It represents the life work of a man of God who has lovingly, selflessly, and authentically poured his life out into many others—me included. Lee's experiences and wisdom, described in *Follow Me*, will ignite an infectious passion in you to fulfill the Great Commission. Lee's book will also give you practical tools to disciple others to do the same. I believe this book will be used around the world as a healthy model of how to multiply a new discipleship movement.

—JOSH LINDQUIST
EVANGELIST, GLOBAL REVIVAL HARVEST
ST. PAUL, MINNESOTA

I've known Lee Grady for several years, and I know everything he has written in this book is a lifestyle for him. His discipleship and mentoring have impacted many, including me—all the way to a distant island in Asia. If you've been stuck in the same place spiritually for many years, or if you've had a hard time influencing others for Christ, this book is for you. *Follow Me* will help you shift relationally, and it will impact your life spiritually in ways you cannot imagine.

—DINESH MICHEL
PRESIDENT, HISTORY MAKER GENERATION
COLOMBO, SRI LANKA

D1562793

Today as never before we need laborers for the end-time harvest. Lee Grady reminds us in this book about the importance of making disciples the Jesus way. He takes us on a journey of his own experiences and through biblical history, giving examples of many great men and women who became followers of Jesus and then raised up other disciples who changed history. Lee makes one thing clear: mass evangelism is not effective unless there is also mass discipleship. True disciples are made through deep, devoted, and sacrificial relationships with those whom God has entrusted to you. This timely book is a great equipping tool for leaders who want to be effective in fulfilling the Great Commission.

—NATASHA SCHEDRIVAYA
EVANGELIST, VILLAGE GOSPEL HARVEST
MOSCOW, RUSSIA

From the first time I met Lee Grady, it was easy to recognize that his whole life centers on discipleship. Lee is the real deal. He doesn't just talk the talk; he walks the walk. And you will find this oozing from the pages of this book as you read story after story of his passion. The church needs to go back to the central command of our Lord Jesus, which is discipleship. It must be the principal work of the church.

—REV. YANG TUCK YOONG
SENIOR PASTOR, CORNERSTONE COMMUNITY CHURCH
SINGAPORE

I can't think of anyone more qualified to write a book on discipleship than Lee Grady. Everywhere Lee goes, young men drive hundreds of miles to be near their trusted mentor. He is a Paul figure in my life too, as he is to hundreds of others across the globe. Lee believes in discipleship and has committed his life to it, and this book is the by-product of that commitment. Don't just read the information; catch the heart behind the message. Go and make disciples!

—DANIEL WEEKS
SENIOR PASTOR, BETHEL CHURCH
GOLDSBORO, NORTH CAROLINA

As one who has been called to preach the gospel to terrorists in conflict zones, often at great risk to my personal safety, I have benefited greatly from Lee Grady's practical approach to discipleship over the course of seventeen years that we have maintained a close friendship. We have ministered together in Africa, Europe, and North America. Many Christians struggle when communicating the gospel to others. Most believers are unsure of how to share the love of Jesus or how to help people grow in the Christian faith. This important book will change the way you follow Jesus by providing practical steps on how to communicate the love of God and help believers thrive and grow spiritually. I highly recommend this transformative book, written by a seasoned man of God who consistently practices what he preaches.

—Rev. Kelechi Okengwu
Evangelist
Umuahia, Abia State, Nigeria

I have benefited greatly from Lee Grady's visits to Singapore, where I have pastored an Indonesian congregation for ten years. I have watched how he invests sacrificially in others as a disciple maker. And I learned an important lesson from Lee when he washed the people's feet while he was preaching here. I began to boldly do this too. This book will show you the power of servant leadership.

—Peter Sam
Pastor, Cornerstone Bahasa Indonesia Fellowship
Singapore

You may think you've picked up a book to read, but you have way more than that with *Follow Me*. In this book you have a window into the life and ministry of my friend Lee Grady. He has lived his message first and written it second. I pray you will be encouraged, blessed, and graced by God to live a life of relational discipleship!

—Chris Friend
National Leader, IPHC Ministries
Perth, Australia

Lee Grady has made it his mission to purposely follow Jesus while also inviting others to follow in his footsteps with true intentionality. Lee has refused to do the work of God's kingdom alone. He's not trying to be a superstar in the church; he is seeking to model true servanthood. Even before this book was written, I was a ripened fruit of this message because Lee's commitment to discipleship has impacted me so personally.

—Antione Ashley
Senior Pastor, Arise Church
DeLand, Florida

I've waited for a book like *Follow Me* for twenty years. But more importantly, I waited many years for the Lord to send me a mentor like Lee Grady, because I needed discipleship as a leader. I needed a safe place to be vulnerable; I needed a friend who would not judge or reject me because of my weaknesses. I know Lee is just a man, but he is a surrendered man who makes himself available to invest in others. Lee's heart bleeds relational discipleship because he wants to see men and women healed, strengthened, and mature so they can make more disciples.

—Michael Coretti
Senior Pastor, Evangel Pentecostal Church
Brantford, Ontario

Not only does Lee Grady write powerful insights in this book, but he lives this message. My leadership style and mindsets have changed as a direct result of the life message Lee carries so well. I absolutely recommend *Follow Me* for any believer who wants to mature. This book has helped me, and I know it will help anyone who wants to become a relational and intentional disciple maker.

—Meesh Fomenko
Evangelist, Be Moved
Ventura, California

Follow Me is a book that is relevant to the twenty-first-century church. I believe it should be in every church leader's library. Lee has written a readable, practical, inspiring book that brings us back to the Great Commission as it was carried out in the Book of Acts. The contrast between Jesus' call to make disciples of all nations and the current church model is brought into sharp focus. I thank God for Lee Grady's humility, emphasis on relationships, and living what he preaches.

—FIONA DES FONTAINE
FORMER SENIOR PASTOR, HIS CHURCH
DURBAN, SOUTH AFRICA

Lee Grady is a humble Bible teacher whose books and messages have impacted people globally. His life and teachings speak volumes about his character and passion for Christ. *Follow Me* will take people through an important process: they will shift from being fans of Jesus to being true followers of Jesus—and then to becoming true influencers. This book will take your personal walk with the Lord to a whole new level.

—RATNA KUMAR SAJJA
SENIOR PASTOR, MESSIAH FELLOWSHIP CHURCH
VIJAYAWADA, INDIA

Follow Me is loaded with gems of truth. It is a must-read for every Christian—especially those who are called to expand their influence. Lee's teachings on discipleship and effective mentoring are not just textbook subjects. He is a man who walks the walk and imparts from his wealth of knowledge and experience. This book is a super-rich manual worth sharing with all churches.

—HAZEIL MIÑOZA
PASTOR, CHURCH PLANTER,
CORNERSTONE COMMUNITY CHURCH
SINGAPORE

If you are looking to make a life-changing impact in the lives of people through relational discipleship, this is the book to study. *Follow Me* is filled with faith-lifting stories, fresh revelation, and practical steps that will empower you to become an effective disciple maker. Over the years, I have watched Lee not only passionately teach on this subject but most importantly live it out daily. You and all the people you will influence will benefit from this important book.

—PAUL HANFERE
PASTOR, OVERFLOW CITY CHURCH
SILVER SPRING, MARYLAND

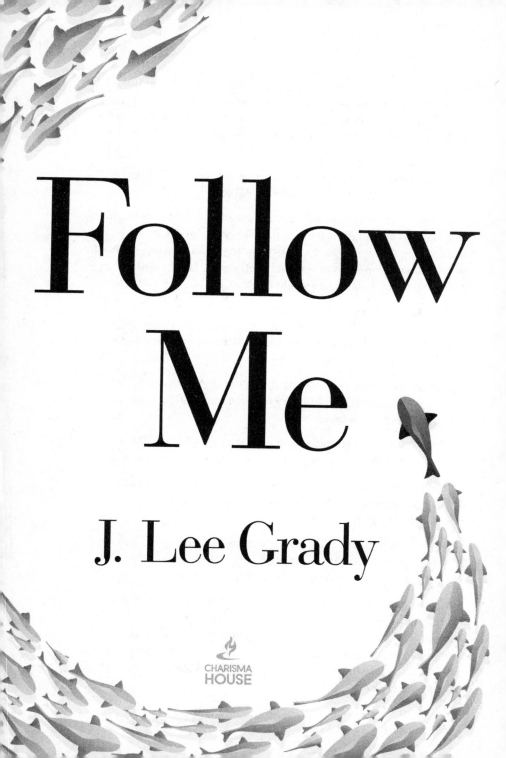

Follow Me

J. Lee Grady

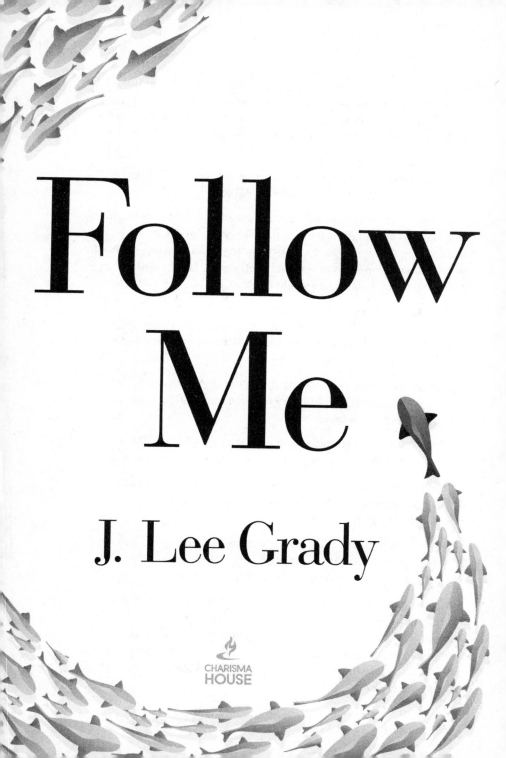

CHARISMA
HOUSE

Back cover photo by Vadim Paripa

Visit the author's website at https://leegrady.com.

Cataloging-in-Publication Data is on file with the Library of Congress.
International Standard Book Number: 978-1-63641-058-6
E-book ISBN: 978-1-63641-059-3

22 23 24 25 26 — 987654321
Printed in the United States of America

To the men and women I have mentored over the years.
I carry you in my heart always.

I thank my God in all my remembrance of you, always
offering prayer with joy in my every prayer for you all.

—PHILIPPIANS 1:3-4

Contents

Author's Note

The Ichthus Symbol

THROUGHOUT THIS BOOK you will notice a symbol that was used by early Christians during the time of the Roman Empire. We call it the *ichthus* or *ichthys* symbol because it is based on the Greek word for *fish*, which in the Greek is spelled ἰχθύς[1] (also ΙΧΟΥΣ). This fish symbol, composed of two simple arcs, reminded believers that Jesus called His disciples to "become fishers of men" (Mark 1:17).

But the ichthus has a much deeper meaning. It was actually a mnemonic tool used to teach the gospel message. When spelled out, the letters for the word *fish* formed an acrostic—*i* (iota) stands for "Jesus," χ (chi) stands for "Christ," θ (theta) stands for "God," ὐ (upsilon) stands for "Son," and ς (sigma) stands for "Savior."[2]

Christians during the first, second, and third centuries AD put this symbol on doors, tombs, and meeting places to remind people that they worshipped Jesus Christ, the Son of God and Savior of the world. If a Christian in those difficult times met a stranger on the road, he or she might scribble one of the arcs in the sand or on a rock, and the other person—if a

Christian—would complete the picture to prove he or she was also a follower of Jesus.[3]

The ichthus is a somber reminder of the price early Christians paid to follow the Messiah in a hostile culture. It is also a powerful symbol of discipleship. Since the day that Jesus invited His disciples to become fishers of men, millions of people have "left their nets" (Matt. 4:20) to follow the Savior—and after being discipled themselves have in turn discipled others. This is the reason the gospel continues to spread throughout the world today. My prayer is that we will take up our crosses and follow Him fully. May we complete the task of discipling all nations in our generation. Come quickly, Lord Jesus!

Foreword

By Barry St. Clair

MORE THAN ANYONE else in my life experience, Lee Grady has understood and practiced the way of Jesus in making disciples. The global influence Lee has had in doing this astounds me, both in the depth of his relationships with his disciples and the breadth of the number of disciples in whom he has invested. They are all over the world!

Though I can take no credit for how the Lord has used Lee to make disciples, I can tell you how it began. Years ago, though a novice in youth ministry, I had discovered that teenagers did not need entertainment and events to follow Jesus but rather relationships in a small-group setting. Yet I had no idea how to do that.

On my first attempt at a discipleship group in 1973, I gathered six fifteen-year-old guys from my church and taught them Bible lessons in my basement in suburban Atlanta. When I asked for questions, all I heard was crickets. After ten weeks of these awkward lessons, I knew my approach was not working.

That insight became very evident when I heard that one young man in our group—Lee Grady—had decided to drop out of church. That was not the outcome I had in mind! When I met with Lee and asked him about his spiritual struggle, he answered, "I am confused." That conversation led to a closer relationship between Lee and me, a fresh restart of our discipleship group, and the beginning of Lee's personal relationship with Jesus.

For the next three years Lee and the others met with me every week to explore who Jesus is and how to follow Him. From then until now Lee and I have shared life together. We did ministry trips, I was a groomsman in his wedding in Florida, and I preached at his ordination in Georgia. He was also visiting me at my house the weekend my first wife, Carol, died.

I also spoke at several of Lee's Bold Venture men's retreats. Recently he and I did tag team speaking at a summit on discipleship, and we offered ourselves as living illustrations that affirmed Jesus' words, "Go and make disciples of all nations." Lee and I spend time together at every opportunity. We laugh and cry, talk and pray, and experience friendship at its deepest level. And I revel at hearing the personal stories of the astounding number of people Lee disciples around the world.

Throughout the years, I have watched Lee follow in Jesus' footsteps as He mentors people. Jesus' course of action led His disciples to experience significant life changes—until they became life changers themselves. I see this four-step pattern in the New Testament:

1. **"I do it."** Jesus never asked His disciples to do anything that He had not done first. He set the pace.

2. **"I do it, and they are with Me."** Jesus always had His disciples with Him except for times when He slipped away to spend time with His Father.

3. **"They do it, and I am with them."** Eventually Jesus sent His disciples out to do what He had been doing, yet He was always close by.

4. **"They do it, and I am in the background to encourage."** When Jesus ascended to the Father, He left the Holy Spirit to give His disciples all they needed to keep on doing what He had been doing.

This kind of reproducing, multiplying disciple making is what changed the world in the first century, and it remains the only way to reach the world with the gospel and change it in the twenty-first century. Lee's book *Follow Me* will give you what you need so that you too can engage in Jesus' ministry of producing life change and life changers!

Investing in Lee Grady's life and Lee's investing in mine stand out as one of my greatest life privileges. What you will read in these pages will convince you to do what Lee Grady has done. Better yet, reading this book and then investing your life in disciple making as Lee does will cause you to spend your time doing exactly what Jesus did!

Barry St. Clair was the founder and director of Reach Out Youth Solutions, an Atlanta-based ministry focused on training youth pastors and leaders. An expert on youth discipleship, he now serves as vice president of Global Youth Engagement for East-West Ministries, based in the Dallas area. St. Clair is the author of numerous books, including Jesus No Equal, Influencing Your World, Following Jesus, Making Jesus Lord, *and* Talking With Your Kids About Love, Sex, and Dating.

DISCIPLESHIP TIP
Be Relational, Not Professional

Imagine the apostle Paul in a cold, dark prison in Rome. His feet may have been chained. His cell may have had rats or mildew. He knew he could die any day, so he thought a lot about heaven. Yet in that awful place he wrote to his disciples in Philippi: "I have you in my heart" (Phil. 1:7). He also said: "How I long for you all with the affection of Christ Jesus" (v. 8). I imagine Paul wept as he penned those words. Yet when we read them today in our Bibles, we don't see the tearstains.

What motivated Paul to pour out his life "as a drink offering" (Phil. 2:17) for others? He had God's deep love for people. This same love is what fuels my passion for discipleship. I feel love and affection for those I mentor. I have their photos in my phone, and I pray for them daily. I call, text, and chat with them on Zoom calls. I meet with them for face-to-face conversations. And yes, the goodbyes are painful. Discipleship isn't clinical, programmatic, or professional. It is warm, relational, and stained with tears. If you want to make disciples as Jesus did, ask Him to put His gigantic heart of love inside you.

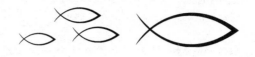

CHAPTER 1

"Follow Me"—the
Call of the Savior

I N EARLY 2020, two months before I ever heard the word *coronavirus*, I stopped at a convenience store near my home in LaGrange, Georgia, to fill up my gas tank. When I went inside to purchase a few items, I noticed the clerk at the cash register had a thick Indian accent. "What part of India are you from?" I asked the man, who looked as if he was in his late forties.

The man seemed surprised that I knew his ethnicity. He asked: "You know India?"

I told him I had visited there four times and that I had good friends in several cities in the states of Andhra Pradesh, Telangana, Maharashtra, Bihar, Tamil Nadu, and Kerala.

"I am from Hyderabad," he told me as he handed me my change.

"Oh, so you speak the Telegu language," I said. Now I had the man's full attention. He couldn't believe a guy from a small town in Georgia knew anything about his country or his regional dialect. He seemed surprised that I cared. He smiled and bobbed his head from side to side in typical Indian fashion.

In that moment all the other customers left the store, and I was able to have a focused conversation with my new friend. I learned that his name is Mahipal, that he has a wife and family back home, and that he grew up in a nominal Christian family.

When I explained that I'm a minister and that I have some close disciples in Hyderabad, he asked me point-blank: "Would you disciple me?"

I can promise you I had never heard those words before while standing at a store counter!

That began a fascinating friendship that grew more interesting when the coronavirus pandemic shut down all my travels and forced most businesses to close. Fortunately for Mahipal, his store was considered an essential business, so it stayed open. And since he worked seven days a week, I started visiting him on most mornings to help him grow in his faith.

A few weeks later he realized he had never actually been born again. Like so many nominal Christians in India, Mahipal went to church only once or twice a year and did not take his faith seriously. He followed a dead religious tradition. So we prayed together at a table in the rear of his store, near the video poker machines. He invited Jesus to take over his life.

Thus began my journey of discipleship with Mahipal. He wore a mask and gloves on the job, and we stayed six feet away from each other to comply with pandemic rules. We greeted each other with elbow bumps instead of hugs. But Mahipal's smile got brighter each day as I shared Christ's love with him as a mentor and friend.

Every morning I would stop at the store to have a coffee and an informal Bible lesson with Mahipal. We talked about prayer, the ministry of the Holy Spirit, and the differences among Matthew, Mark, Luke, and John. (When we first started our Bible studies, he assumed that John the Baptist wrote John's Gospel.) Mahipal often had to run to the counter to sell cigarettes, beer, or lottery tickets to customers, but then he rushed back to read another Bible verse or to ask another question. This went on for months.

One day we began talking about the importance of water baptism, and Mahipal asked if he could be baptized. Most churches weren't having in-person services at that time, but a pastor I knew offered to fill the baptismal tank in his church on a Sunday afternoon. I invited about ten friends, and they distanced themselves all over the sanctuary and wore masks. I got tearful when Mahipal stood in the water and testified that Jesus Christ is the only true God. His boss, who was a Hindu, was watching from the back of the church.

I call this my "pandemic miracle" because I never would have expected to take on such an important ministry assignment when the world was in total lockdown. Mahipal helped me understand that even during a world crisis when people were sheltering in place, God was still drawing people to Himself. The Holy Spirit is never in quarantine.

After Mahipal's baptism, I shared with him about the importance of being baptized in the Holy Spirit. Being unfamiliar with the biblical term, he thought we needed to fill up the baptismal tank again with water for a second dunk! I explained to him that we only needed to pray and that God would fill him with the Holy Spirit and anoint him for ministry. We prayed together the next week in his backyard on a hot Georgia afternoon, and Mahipal was gloriously filled with the Spirit's power and boldness as he sat in a lawn chair.

The next day I got a text from Mahipal. He said: "Can you follow up with this person? I just prayed with him to receive Jesus." He had led a man to Christ in the gas station!

Over the course of the next few months, Mahipal prayed with eleven people to become Christians. In each case they were paying for cigarettes or other items, and he started a conversation with them about faith while they were standing at the cash register. One lady who was buying cigarettes even began crying as she prayed with my friend.

A few more months went by, and Mahipal realized he needed to go home to India to tend to his family there. Before we said our goodbyes, he told me his plan. "Pastor Lee, when I get back to Hyderabad I am going to invite all my nominal Christian friends and my Hindu friends to my house for a meal. I am going to share my testimony with them and tell how I was born again in America. I want to lead many people to Jesus when I return," he said.

I encouraged Mahipal to watch some old Billy Graham sermons on YouTube so he could learn how to present the gospel message clearly. And the day I took him to the Atlanta airport to fly home, I prayed with Mahipal's Hindu boss to become a Christian. The man who had watched the baptism from the back of the church in May decided to follow Jesus too.

A chain reaction of grace had started before Mahipal arrived home on the other side of the world.

It is impossible for me to fully express the joy I feel when I see how this dear Indian brother is following Christ today. We talk often on video calls. He got connected to a healthy church in Hyderabad, and he is growing spiritually.

I didn't know I would meet him when I went into a gas station in early 2020 to purchase a bottle of water. I had no idea that this chance encounter at Exit 14 off Interstate 85 in Georgia would lead to hours and hours of discipleship meetings in his store. And I had no clue that this seemingly soft-spoken man with a thick foreign accent would end up going back to India to lead others to Christ.

This story demonstrates the power of relational discipleship. When you influence one person for Jesus, it triggers a domino effect. It starts small, but the impact builds over time. It's possible that hundreds of people in India will find Christ because I spent time studying the Book of Mark with one Indian convert in the back of a convenience store in Georgia. After God uses you in a situation like the one I've just described, you will want to spend the rest of your life making disciples. His using me in this way is the reason discipleship has become my passion. And the need for every believer to make disciples is the reason the message of this book is so important.

Jesus Began With a Few

My wife and I had the opportunity to tour Israel with a small group of friends in 2018. I'll never forget walking along the rocky shore of the Sea of Galilee, looking out at the small fishing boats and imagining what it would have been like to see Jesus and His small group of disciples in that place, just a few miles south of Capernaum.

When I got close to the water I rolled up my pants to my knees and waded in. I noticed some fishermen throwing their nets into the blue waters. I closed my eyes and tried to visualize a young Peter and his brother, Andrew, as they dragged their boat out from the shore and threw their nets on the waves. Fishing had been their daily routine for a long time. But one special day Jesus showed up and called to them from the water's edge, *"Follow Me, and I will make you become fishers of men"* (Mark 1:17, emphasis added).

Peter and Andrew didn't fully understand what Jesus meant when He issued that strange invitation. But they knew He was a rabbi, and they understood that He was inviting them to leave their mundane jobs on the water and begin a new spiritual adventure. They didn't hesitate. Mark 1:18 says, "Immediately they left their nets and followed him."

That same day Jesus invited James and John, the sons of Zebedee, to join His small group. The four men went with Jesus to the local synagogue, where Jesus' sermon was suddenly interrupted by the tortured cries of a demon-possessed man. The demon screamed at Jesus: "I know who you are—the Holy One of God!" (Mark 1:24). Then Jesus commanded the evil spirit to leave, and the man was thrown into convulsions before the demon screamed again and left the man's body (vv. 25–26).

Can you imagine what Peter, Andrew, James, and John were thinking during this chaotic scene? "What are we doing here? Is every day going to be like this? How did Jesus do that?" But the four men stayed close to Jesus as they left the synagogue and walked to Peter's house nearby.

Everyone in Capernaum was talking about Jesus that day— and the four young disciples were now part of the action. The townspeople were saying, "He commands even the unclean spirits, and they obey Him!" (Mark 1:27). But Jesus didn't do this amazing feat alone—He had His four friends with Him. His new companions were a part of this bold mission.

That evening at Peter's house, Jesus healed Peter's mother-in-law from a fever (Mark 1:29–31). Jesus' powerful ministry became very personal to Peter that day. As soon as word got out about that miracle, everyone from the city was at the door. Family and friends brought their sick loved ones to be healed, and others were delivered from demons (vv. 32–34).

Peter's house suddenly became ground zero for something wonderful. The next morning, when Peter went to tell Jesus that more people were looking for Him, Jesus said these words: "Let us go somewhere else to the towns nearby, so that I may preach there also; for that is what I came for" (Mark 1:38).

Notice Jesus did not say, "*I* need to go to some other towns" or "People need *Me* over in Nazareth or in Samaria." He said to Peter, "Let *us* go." Jesus did not see the mission as His alone. *He wanted His followers to join Him.* They were His team. He had every intention of including them in His quest.

These beautiful scenes show us the essence of biblical discipleship. Jesus came to save the world, and He invites us to join Him in His work. Of course we don't have the power to save people from sin. We are flawed vessels of clay. Yet He calls us to be His coworkers—to walk with Him, to feel what He feels, and to be a part of His audacious mission to change the whole world.

He wants to do His work through us.

When Jesus issued His original invitation to Peter, He said: "Follow Me, and I will make you become fishers of men" (Mark 1:17). Jesus' mission is to "catch" as many "fish" as possible—but He does this by training men and women to be His workforce. If we choose to follow Him, we must go through a process of growth and training.

You don't become a fisher of men overnight. Jesus said, "I will *make you become*..." (emphasis added). He invites us to enroll in a supernatural process of spiritual formation. When we submit to that process we become more like Him, and we begin to do

His work in His way. We become true disciples who carry His heart, reflect His character, and complete His mission.

Peter went through quite a process. From the moment Jesus moved into his house, this fisherman had a front-row seat as the gospel story unfolded. He watched the healing of paralytics, lepers, and bleeding women; he listened closely to Jesus' teachings as the disciples walked along the dusty roads; he heard the Pharisees question Jesus and listened in amazement as Jesus rebuked them.

At one point Jesus even called Peter out of the boat to walk with Him on the water (Matt. 14:28–29). In another instance Jesus told Peter to go and find a coin in a fish's mouth (17:27). And after Jesus fed a multitude with just a few scraps of food, He asked Peter: "But who do you say that I am?" and Peter gave the right answer: "You are the Christ" (Mark 8:29). Peter was well on his way to becoming a leader among Jesus' followers. He was probably the first of Jesus' followers to realize that Jesus was the Messiah.

The training got more rigorous after Jesus called the three men in His inner circle—Peter, James, and John—to see His heavenly glory on the Mount of Transfiguration. Peter stared in awe as Moses and Elijah conversed with Jesus and a cloud of shining glory covered them. The three uneducated fishermen, with their jaws dropping, were given the chance to see things that angels have longed to see for ages. They beheld the Messiah in His heavenly glory and realized He is the focal point of all history (Matt. 17:1–8).

All this was part of a divine preparation process. But Jesus didn't allow these lofty revelations to puff Peter up with pride; before Jesus' crucifixion, Peter came face to face with his own soul-crushing weakness. In a moment of intense temptation, Peter almost crossed over to the dark side.

The night Jesus was arrested, Peter was stressed to the breaking point and fearful of the crowd. When the high priest's servant girl accused him of being a disciple of Jesus, he denied it (Mark 14:66–68, MEV). When the girl repeated her accusation to some bystanders, Peter denied knowing Jesus again (vv. 69–70). When others questioned him, Peter "began to invoke a curse on himself, and to swear, 'I do not know this Man of whom you speak'" (v. 71, MEV). The brave disciple who had promised Jesus he would follow Him anywhere turned into a pitiful wimp. He caved under the pressure. When the rooster crowed, Peter remembered Jesus' words: "Before the rooster crows twice, you will deny Me three times" (v. 72, MEV).

This could have been the end for Peter. He wept bitterly and disappeared (Mark 14:72). No words beyond his denial are recorded in Matthew's and Mark's Gospels. In the Gospel of Luke, we read that Peter went to Jesus' tomb and found it empty. John's Gospel is the only one that describes how Peter found full restoration after his failure.

Sulking, lonely and dejected, Peter went back to what he knew—his boring fishing job. He had fished all night and caught nothing (John 21:3). Perhaps he feared that God had rejected him forever. But then Jesus appeared on the shore and invited His friends to cast their nets on the right side of the boat—and they hauled in a full net of fish (v. 6).

This was a divine sign that their Master still had plans to use Peter in spite of his cowardly denials. Peter must have been curious when he saw the smoke from the charcoal fire Jesus had made on the beach. How could this be? Jesus wasn't frowning or scowling. Nor was He waiting to deliver a stern rebuke. He didn't scold Peter or even remind him of his cowardly denial. This amazing Savior simply invited Peter to sit with Him and eat a hot breakfast. Jesus wanted to eat grilled fish with His friend and chat with him by the warmth of that fire (John 21:9–13).

Before that breakfast conversation ended, Jesus repeated some important words that Peter had heard a few years earlier on that same rocky shoreline.

Jesus said again, "Follow Me" (John 21:19).

Jesus had not disqualified Peter! He was renewing His invitation. The broken, unstable man whom Jesus nicknamed a "rock" was not sent away (Matt. 16:18). He was back in the game. Jesus had taken His beloved friend through a rigorous training process that included an embarrassing failure. But on that day He reaffirmed that He would use Peter to "catch" many souls and reproduce the life of God in people.

What is even more amazing is the way the shaky, impetuous, insecure Peter was transformed after he was baptized in the Holy Spirit a few weeks later in the Upper Room in Jerusalem. This weak man, who crumbled under pressure when his Master was arrested, then preached the gospel to a huge crowd—and three thousand people made decisions to follow the Messiah (Acts 2:14–41).

Jesus did exactly what He said He would: *He made Peter a fisher of men.*

This is what God wants to do to you—and to every follower of Christ. Just as Peter had to be transformed, so you too must go through a process to become a disciple maker. Don't focus on your flaws or failures; grace will change you. When you read Peter's first epistle you see that he became an apostle and a strong spiritual father to his followers (1 Pet. 1:1). Peter wrote this letter to "newborn babies," and he challenged them to "grow" (2:2). Jesus had miraculously changed Peter from a weak man into a powerful influencer who nurtured and mentored others.

I have seen this pattern unfold in my own life. As I grew spiritually, God began to bring people into my life, and I helped them grow.

Many years ago I met a young man named Paul Muzichuk at a conference in Florida. Paul was born in Ukraine, but he came to the United States as a young boy and grew up in Russian-speaking churches. He had a huge passion for God, but he lacked direction because mentoring and discipleship are rare in the Slavic Christian context. When Paul talked to me I could sense he had a hunger to be trained.

I invited Paul to breakfast during that conference, and he admits to this day that he couldn't believe I wanted to meet with him. In fact, when I invited him, he didn't think I was serious. No leader in his circle ever paid much attention to young people. I saw potential in this young man, and I wanted to encourage him. Little did I know that our friendship would grow and he would eventually travel with me on more than two dozen trips to many cities in the United States as well as to Hungary, Romania, and Colombia.

Eventually Paul came to work for me as my ministry administrator while he was working part-time for his church in Florida. When we were together, Paul would pick my brain constantly for leadership tips or insights into Scripture. We would stay up late during ministry trips talking about how God moved in the meetings and what we learned from various challenges. I knew Paul was watching me, not only while I was preaching but also when I experienced disappointment or criticism or when I was facing financial challenges.

Before long I found myself giving Paul the microphone and letting him preach in my ministry events. I will never forget the night he preached to a group of men in Maryland about how God taught him to forgive some people who treated him unjustly. There is no greater feeling of fulfillment than when you see your spiritual children growing up and acting like Jesus!

I can't take credit for Paul's maturity, but I know the Lord allowed me to play a small role in helping him grow as a leader. Paul eventually was asked to take a full-time pastoral position with his church in Florida, and I had to cut the umbilical cord and release him to bless others. This is one of the most difficult things about discipleship—we must let people go. They can't stay in the nest forever. But my friendship with Paul remains strong to this day.

During the past few years I have had the amazing privilege of mentoring many young leaders like Paul: there's Clem, a Chinese guy from Australia who shares his faith with students as well as members of the medical community; Robert, a pastor in Uganda who has established a thriving school for needy kids as well as a women's shelter; Billy, a young Filipino living in Singapore who is now leading a congregation of Filipino immigrants; Khuram, a Pakistani American who has founded an Urdu church in Baltimore; and Alex, a businessman who leads the men's discipleship ministry in his church in Romania.

Jesus made me a fisher of men, just as He did Peter. My influence has expanded beyond my wildest dreams simply because Jesus showed me how to invest in people. I believe this is what Jesus was referring to when He promised us abundant life in John 10:10. There is nothing more rewarding than meaningful relationships.

Peter had a special bond with the people he mentored. And at the end of his first epistle he mentions his "son," Mark (1 Pet. 5:13). This is the same Mark who wrote the Gospel of Mark! Peter had the privilege of discipling a young man who gave us one of the four Gospels. God can give you disciples who will reach far more people than you do. When you choose to follow Jesus, He will make you a person of *transforming influence.*

LET'S **PRAY** ABOUT IT

Lord, make me a fisher of men. You did it with Peter two thousand years ago. Do it again with me. Take me through Your holy process so I can reproduce Your life in others. Direct my steps so that I will meet people who need Jesus. Give me the boldness to share the message of Christ with them and the patience to mentor them in the faith. Amen.

ONE **FINAL** THOUGHT

Every true believer born into the family of God has the potential of being a reproducer.[1]

–Dawson Trotman, Founder, The Navigators

DISCIPLESHIP TIP
Leave a Permanent Mark!

When you disciple someone, you set an example. You are showing them how to live the Christian life. You are saying, "Follow me. Watch how I do it. Let me show you what I've learned." Paul told the Corinthians, "Be imitators of me, just as I also am of Christ" (1 Cor. 11:1). Paul told the Thessalonians that he, Silvanus, and Timothy had offered themselves "as a *model* for you, so that you would follow our example" (2 Thess. 3:9, emphasis added).

The word for *model* in 2 Thessalonians 3:9 is the Greek word *typos*, which means "the mark of a stroke or blow, print" or "a figure formed by a blow or impression."[1] When you mentor someone, you leave a permanent mark on his or her life through your prayers, love, and instruction. This mark is made not only by your words but also by your actions. When you pour your life sacrificially into your disciples, they will never forget what you did for them. Through the Holy Spirit's power, you are leaving an unforgettable impression. This is my prayer for you: that you will leave a permanent mark on those you mentor!

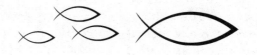

CHAPTER 2

God Wants You to Be an Influencer

THE KUMBH MELA pilgrimage, a Hindu festival held at one of four spots along the Ganges River in India every three years, is believed to be one of the largest gatherings in the world. The festival at Prayagraj, Uttar Pradesh, has become the largest. In 2013 an estimated 30 million people attended that event in one day.[2] Rock star Rod Stewart's free beachside concert in Rio de Janeiro on New Year's Eve 1994—which supposedly attracted 4.2 million people, if you include those who showed up just for the fireworks concert at midnight—is believed to be the largest concert ever held.[3]

Did either of these gatherings change your life? I doubt it.

When we think of influence, our carnal minds always tend to drift toward big numbers. In fact, we have a phenomenon today called "internet influencers." These are people who have huge followings on Instagram, Twitter, or other social media platforms. They are basically famous for being famous, even though what they do on social media is quite trivial. For example, some influencers are famous because of the way they apply makeup, design fingernails, or share endless photos of themselves lifting weights or modeling swimwear.

One of the biggest personalities on social media in 2021 was

James Charles, a guy who became famous for creatively applying neon-colored eye shadow and mascara. When he was only nineteen, he became the first male spokesmodel for *Cover Girl*,[4] and as of this writing he has nearly two and a half million followers on Facebook and more than twenty-six million on Instagram. But if you have never heard of James Charles, you are not alone. Just because he has a big following doesn't mean he has made an eternal difference.

Jesus attracted big crowds, but the numbers didn't impress Him because He knew many who were healed in His meetings wouldn't follow Him after He went to the cross. He told the people in His audience that the gospel seeds He was sowing would be eaten by birds, scorched and withered, or choked by thorns. Only a small percentage, He said, would actually bear fruit. (See Mark 4:3–8.)

Jesus was looking for *quality*, not *quantity*.

In the end, after thousands of people heard Jesus' messages and ate His free lunches, only 120 of His followers gathered in the Upper Room on the day of Pentecost. That is not an impressive number, and today's church growth specialists might note that Jesus failed to break the 200 barrier within three years of ministry!

There are a few crowd shots in the Book of Acts. But most scenes of the early church are less impressive. A single Ethiopian man was converted on a desert road (Acts 8:26–38). The Holy Spirit fell on members of an Italian family gathered in a home in Caesarea (Acts 10:30–33, 44). A woman named Lydia came to Christ at a small prayer gathering by a river in Philippi, becoming the first convert in Europe (Acts 16:14).

Why are these seemingly inconsequential stories highlighted in Scripture? Because God moves as powerfully in one-on-one conversations and small-group gatherings as He does in big meetings. When we follow the cloud of His presence, He often leads us to the one instead of the many. He defines influence differently than we do.

The Book of Acts ends with a scene of Paul ministering quietly to people in a small apartment while he is under house arrest (Acts 28:30–31). Paul certainly didn't measure his impact by large buildings, big mailing lists, media exposure, or book sales. Paul never led a megachurch with ten satellite campuses. And his writings didn't become popular until long after he was dead. It would seem that Paul's seed had to die in the ground before it sprouted anew.

We need to stop evaluating our own effectiveness—and each other's—by crowd size or popularity. If you are a leader, be faithful with the people you have, whether it is a home church of seven, a campus Bible study of ten, a rural congregation of thirty, or a megachurch of two thousand. Whether you are ministering to a handful of inmates, a roomful of Alzheimer's patients, a dozen orphans, or one depressed friend, forget your need for the spotlight. If God has called you to invest in third-graders in an inner city school, drug addicts in a rehab facility, or students in a rural community college, thank God for your sphere of influence and plant your spiritual seeds there.

Jesus gave us a refreshingly different perspective on crowd size. He told His disciples: "For where two or three have gathered together in My name, I am there in their midst" (Matt. 18:20). If He loves small gatherings, why should we despise them? In the kingdom of God, influence is measured differently than it is in this fallen, narcissistic world. We need to be delivered from worshipping "big." Instead of striving for attention and focusing on size, we must invest in a few. We plant small seeds, and then we watch as our small impact multiplies.

God's Plan for Multiplication

God told Adam and Eve: "Be fruitful and multiply, and fill the earth" (Gen. 1:28). Jesus restated this command when He gave what we call the Great Commission: "Go therefore and make disciples" (Matt. 28:19). The Creator formed the first man out of clay, breathed life into him, and commissioned him to procreate; Jesus, who was God in the flesh, breathed the breath of His Spirit into His disciples (John 20:22) and then commanded them to multiply. The life giver has given us the divine mandate to impart His life into others so that His kingdom can advance.

From the beginning of the Bible to the end we see this principle of multiplication through close mentoring relationships. Moses discipled Joshua. Naomi discipled Ruth. Mordecai discipled Esther. Elijah discipled Elisha.

After David became king he trained thirty-seven men who became famous warriors. The Bible calls them "mighty men," and their names are listed in 2 Samuel 23. It seems the same anointing that was on David came upon his mighty warriors. They were exceptionally loyal, strong, and brave. Among them were Adino, Eleazar, and Shammah. (They were called "the three" because their victories were legendary. Similarly, Jesus had three men among His disciples—Peter, James, and John—who walked in exceptional power.)

David's mighty men remind me that God did not anoint me just so I can have a ministry. No, He wants me to share my anointing by discipling others. He wants me to reproduce. God wants you to do the same. As you spend time with your disciples, encourage them, train them, advise them, pray for them, and take them with you on ministry assignments—they will become legends.

Elijah was a mighty prophet. He multiplied food and oil, raised a child from the dead, ended a drought, and even called fire down from heaven more than once. (See 1 Kings 17:13–16, 17–23; 18:36–38, 41–45; and 2 Samuel 1:10, 12.) But Elijah didn't want his ministry to end with him. He was focused on the next generation. He had schools of young prophets in at least six locations (see 2 Kings 2:3, 5, 7),[5] and he invested much of his time training Elisha, who followed him more closely than any of the other young prophets. (See 1 Kings 19:19–21.)

Elijah's legacy didn't stop when he went to heaven in his flaming chariot. His disciple Elisha was so hungry for God that he asked for a "double portion" of his mentor's mantle. (See 2 Kings 2:9, 12.) After Elijah departed from this earth, Elisha ended up performing twice as many miracles as his mentor.[6] And though

Elijah started the process of ending Jezebel's reign of terror, Elisha anointed King Jehu to finish the job. (See 2 Kings 9:1–3.)

This Elijah/Elisha model continued into the New Testament. Though Jesus certainly preached to crowds, He focused most of His attention on twelve men and a small group of women disciples (some of the women's names are mentioned in Luke 8:1–3). The disciples had full access to Jesus; He did not keep them at arm's length or use them as servants. Jesus ate, talked, fished, played, and shared close quarters with His disciples—and He imparted everything He had to them.

If we are going to change people for Christ, we must do it the way Jesus did. We must invest in the few.

In today's church we measure our success by big buildings, by the numbers who sit in our padded chairs, and by how much money pours into the offering plate. The early disciples had a different standard. They measured the effectiveness of their ministry by the maturity of their disciples—and by the impact those disciples had on the people around them.

They didn't measure attendance. They looked for fruit. They expected true disciples of Jesus to reproduce.

During one of Paul's missionary trips, he went to the Greek city of Troas because "a door was opened for me in the Lord" (2 Cor. 2:12). With a population of one hundred thousand, Troas was a huge harvest field. But when Paul arrived there, he became upset. He said: "I had no rest for my spirit, not finding Titus my brother" (v. 13). Paul then left Troas to find his beloved disciple, Titus, in Macedonia. Why would Paul walk away from such a big opportunity in Troas to find one person?

Paul left that place because one mature disciple maker was more valuable to him than a huge crowd. After a long season of training, Titus had become like a son to Paul. Titus was a multiplier, and Paul knew Titus would reach many people even after Paul was gone. So Paul left the big city to find the one.

Many preachers today care about applause, big auditoriums, and the number of clicks on their social media posts, but they don't know how to lift, encourage, and train the one. We need to adopt Paul's priorities. If you invest in one Titus, his multiplied impact will last long after the crowds have lost interest.

Notice the illustration below. I call this the "Concentric Circles of Influence." This was Jesus' method of transformation. He had an inner circle of disciples—Peter, James, and John. Then He had the small group of twelve male disciples, along with an undisclosed number of women disciples mentioned in Luke 8:1–3. Jesus spent most of His time training these individuals to carry on His work.

CONCENTRIC CIRCLES OF INFLUENCE

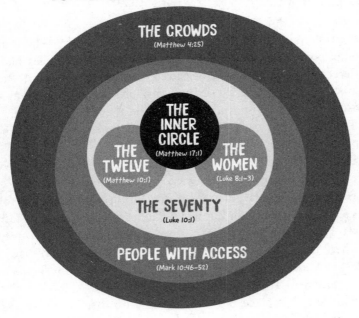

Outside these circles, Jesus had a group of close followers who were known as "the seventy," mentioned in Luke 10:1. (Some early manuscripts list the number as seventy-two.) Jesus obviously spent a lot of time with these people, and He trained them to heal the sick and cast out demons. They might be considered a small ministry school that Jesus organized, somewhat comparable to the schools of the prophets that Elijah formed.

Jesus sent His trainees out into the nearby cities of Israel to preach (Luke 10:1). I can imagine that many of these people ate with Jesus, had direct access to Him, and had the chance to ask Him questions, even though they were not as intimately acquainted with Him as His closest disciples were.

Beyond these circles of influence we see that many individuals had powerful encounters with Jesus. These would have included Bartimaeus, the blind beggar (Mark 10:46–52); Jesus' close friend Lazarus (John 11:43–44); the nameless Samaritan woman (John 4:7–30); Mary and Martha, Lazarus' sisters (Luke 10:38–42); the bleeding woman mentioned in Mark 5:25–34; and Zacchaeus, who repented of his financial corruption after Jesus visited his house for a meal (Luke 19:1–10). The Bible doesn't say these people followed Jesus as closely as His core disciples, but they obviously believed in Him and shared His impact on their lives with others. In fact, the Samaritan woman influenced a whole village to believe that Jesus was the Messiah.

On the outer fringes of the diagram we see the crowds. We know Jesus preached to big audiences in Galilee and beyond. In some cases He healed many sick people, and in two cases He multiplied food supernaturally so that everyone got a free lunch of bread and fish. Jesus even ventured outside the borders of Israel a few times to minister to non-Jews.

When we look at the Bible through our twenty-first-century lenses, we assume that crowd ministry was Jesus' main focus. That's not true. Yes, Jesus did cast His gospel seeds to the masses, knowing that some seed would fall on good soil and that many seeds would be wasted on hard ground. But Jesus found fertile ground in His most devoted followers. He knew crowds are fickle and that the same people who ate His free lunches or stood in His healing lines would eventually demand that He be crucified. Jesus focused on personal relationships, not nameless crowds.

Relational discipleship was the apostle Paul's method of

ministry as well. While he did sometimes speak in larger church meetings or to a crowd of skeptics in Athens (Acts 17:22–31), his ministry was not focused on events, sermons, or a flashy delivery style. Paul did nothing for the cameras; there were no theatrics or gimmicks. And Paul was certainly not interested in high-pressure offerings, pulpit mannerisms, or how many people swooned at the altar.

The apostle's definition of ministry is found in 1 Thessalonians 2:8: "Having so fond an affection for you, we were well-pleased to impart to you not only the gospel of God but also our own lives, because you had become very dear to us." Like Jesus, Paul was all about relationships. He didn't just bring a good sermon; he invested his life in people.

Paul did not live for fawning crowds. He would have hated the celebrity style of ministry we have created in the twenty-first century. The reason he could endure beatings, shipwrecks, betrayal, riots, hunger, and imprisonment is that he loved the men and women on his ministry team. He too had an inner circle and a close group of committed disciples.

Everything Paul did was about pouring the life of Jesus into Timothy, Silvanus, Mark, Phoebe, Epaphras, Luke, Onesimus, Priscilla, Barnabas, Euodia, Syntyche, and all the other New Testament heroes who called Paul a spiritual father. And Paul is described in the Bible as our example. In 1 Corinthians 11:1 Paul writes: "Be imitators of me, just as I also am of Christ." If we are not imitating Paul's methodology, we are not obeying God's discipleship mandate.

When Paul wrote to the Thessalonians he reminded them how this principle of influence works. He said:

> For our gospel did not come to you in word only, but also in power and in the Holy Spirit and with full conviction; just as you know what kind of men we proved to be among you for your sake. You also became imitators of us and of the Lord, having received the word in much

tribulation with the joy of the Holy Spirit, so that you became an example to all the believers in Macedonia and in Achaia.

—1 THESSALONIANS 1:5–7

Notice that the Thessalonians first listened to the gospel message and became imitators of Paul and his team members. Then the same people who imitated Paul became an example to other Christians. The Thessalonians did not stay in spiritual infancy; they grew up! They matured and began influencing others. This is always God's plan.

Walter A. Henrichsen, author of *Disciples Are Made Not Born*, said it this way: "Twelve sons were born to the patriarch Jacob. The Bible tells us that they multiplied and filled the land of Egypt....Jesus chose twelve men to become His 'spiritual children.' He invested three years of His life in them and told them to become fruitful, to multiply, and to spread the gospel to every creature. You and I are Christians today because twelve men caught Jesus' vision and did as He commanded. Spiritual reproduction works!"[7]

Seven Reasons We Don't Make Disciples

Way back in 2008 I had a very scary birthday with a zero in it. I dreaded turning fifty because that number sounded so old! But I chose to accept reality. I also decided I would spend the rest of my life investing in the next generation because I believe discipleship is at the very heart of the gospel.

God began to put young people in my life, and many of them asked me if I would mentor them. I started taking some of them on mission trips. Others called me for counsel or coaching. Some needed prayer to overcome habits or addictions.

The more I invested in them, the more excited I got about helping other Christians grow in their faith. In those early days I spent a lot of time investing in young men like AJ, whom I took with me on a trip to Bolivia; Felipe, a Brazilian immigrant who

FOLLOW ME

eventually began making disciples on his own; Antione, who is now a pastor in Florida; and David, an Indian American who leads evangelistic campaigns on college campuses.

Mentoring young people is the most fulfilling thing I do. I enjoy preaching to crowds, but if I have to choose between speaking to an audience of a thousand or talking to a small group of spiritually hungry young leaders, I would choose the latter every time. That's because relational discipleship is the lost art of Jesus and the secret of New Testament ministry.

Today I believe the Holy Spirit is drawing the church back to the New Testament model. Leaders as well as churchgoers are weary of the impersonal, performance-based, people-in-the-pews approach. We are tired of the show. We have not been called to entertain an audience—we have been commissioned to train an army.

We all know Jesus spent most of His ministry investing in a small number of followers who then invested in others. So why don't we use that approach? Here are seven obvious reasons we don't do it:

1. We are ignorant of the Great Commission.

When Jesus was about to leave this earth, He gave us our final marching orders in Matthew 28:19. He did not say, "Go and attract crowds" or "Go and preach to multitudes" or "Go and build churches." There is certainly nothing wrong with buildings, good sermons, or mass evangelism, but Jesus made it clear that our priority is relational discipleship: "Go and make disciples." If He spent three and a half years investing in a small handful of followers, why do we think we can do it a different way?

2. We have not been discipled ourselves.

It is impossible to mentor someone if you haven't been mentored. Yet countless pastors have admitted to me that they never had a mentor. Bible colleges and seminaries teach theology and methodology, but ministers cannot be mass-produced on an assembly line. God's servants are handmade. They need someone they can talk to, ask questions of, and watch from the front row.

Doctors in this country must go through an intensive internship program, but rarely do Christian leaders receive hands-on training from caring mentors. Paul told the Corinthians, "I became your father through the gospel" (1 Cor. 4:15), but this concept is foreign today because the fatherlessness of our culture is also rampant in the church. We must recover the lost art of mentoring.

3. We prefer programs rather than relationships.

When Jesus called His disciples, He appointed them "*so that they would be with Him* and that He could send them out to preach" (Mark 3:14, emphasis added). Jesus' first desire was for a relationship; the work of the ministry was secondary. Today we have switched priorities—our focus is on the work, and the importance of relationships is minimized or ignored. One pastor recently told me that in his denomination, ministry has been reduced to what he called "the ABCs of attendance, buildings, and cash." When ministry becomes a business, you know you have abandoned true discipleship.

4. We are impressed with size.

The descendants of Noah built the Tower of Babel because they wanted to make a monument to themselves. (See Genesis 11:4.) This has always been the tendency of carnal men. We love big. We love towers and visibility because they stroke our pride. But God came down and confused the builders of Babel because He wanted them to build *out*, not *up*. (See verses 5–9.) We prefer tall monuments to our own glory, but God wants our influence to spread in an outward direction. We prefer *vertical*; God prefers *horizontal*.

Dawson Trotman, the founder of The Navigators organization, was committed to the concept of discipleship because he knew if he could invest in a small group of Christians until they reached maturity, they would then invest in others, and the chain reaction would create a multiplication effect. If four people discipled four other people over a six-month period, Trotman said, and those people discipled four more people in six months, this would result in 1,024 disciples after five years. And after sixteen years, there would be more than two billion disciples![8] If we did it God's way, we could reach the world.

Walter Henrichsen offers a similar example. Suppose an evangelist leads 1,000 people to Jesus every day. That would be 365,000 people every year. That sounds so impressive! Meanwhile, suppose you led just one person to Jesus a year and discipled that person, and then that person discipled one person the following year. At the end of the second year you would have only four disciples.[9] Not too exciting, right?

But if this trend continued, you would end up reaching more than 365,000 people by the nineteenth year—and the number would continue to multiply. You would end up reaching more people than the evangelist, and all those people would be personally discipled—with spiritual maturity and stability to prove it.

5. We lack patience for the process.

Spending three years leading a small group seems unimpressive. There is nothing glamorous or sensational about discipleship. Yet this is exactly what Jesus did—and one of His closest disciples, Peter, ended up denying Him. (See Matthew 26:69–75.) Judas, meanwhile, left the group and hanged himself. (See Matthew 27:5.) Many of us would have given up in those circumstances.

You may get frustrated because some of your disciples flake out or grow at a snail's pace. But you never know the impact your disciples will make in the end. After all, Peter rejoined Jesus' team after he was forgiven and restored. (See John 21:15–17.) Sometimes those who suffer the biggest failures experience the biggest comebacks.

In today's church we want everything fast and easy; yet the Jesus way requires time and may not look impressive at first. You will have to wait for the fruit, and it might not be completely evident until after you are dead. But we can trust God that the seed of His Word will not return void.

6. Our personal brokenness prevents us from healing others.

The process of discipleship includes the healing of our souls from past wounds. We cannot be mature in Christ if we are still bound by sinful habits. Yet many Christians today are stuck in spiritual infancy because they have not gone through the necessary process of healing so they can walk in holiness. You will never bring others to spiritual maturity if you have not learned to overcome your own brokenness.

7. We want churchgoers to stay immature.

When children grow up, they leave their homes, get married, and have their own families. This has been God's plan since He told Adam and Eve to "be fruitful and multiply" (Gen. 1:28). Jesus repeated this commission to His disciples when He said, "My Father is glorified by this, that you bear much fruit, and so prove to be My disciples" (John 15:8). Real disciples make disciples. They don't just sit in church year after year like spectators.

Some insecure pastors don't want members of their congregations to grow because they feel threatened by mature believers. They are afraid someone will steal their ministry. That's crazy! I want my spiritual sons and daughters to surpass me in spiritual fruitfulness. If we are committed to biblical discipleship, we must swallow our pride and get back to the primacy of investing in relationships.

Here's an example of how multiplied influence works. More than fifteen years ago I began mentoring a Slavic guy named Alex Novik. His father came to this country from Belarus many years ago when Alex was a boy because of religious persecution under the Soviet regime. Alex reached out to me for mentoring when he was a young man in his twenties, and I began visiting his Slavic church in Philadelphia. When he started his graphic design business, I gave him a small cash offering. He told me I was his first investor!

Before long I had a new set of young friends with long Russian names like Alex Ankudovich, Dmitry Kolesnikovich, Ruslan Romanov, Eugene Kolomoytsev, Olga Maksimchuk, and Vitaly Vitorsky, his wife, Alesya, and his brother, Gennady. Not only did I learn a lot about Slavic culture and food by hanging around this church, but I also became a part of these young people's lives.

In some cases I performed their weddings; I also prayed for the birth of their children and offered counsel and prayer when they were going through difficult times. We enjoyed retreats together in the Smoky Mountains in Tennessee.

During one of my many visits to the Philadelphia church, I met a man named Ulan Karypov, who was an immigrant from the Central Asian nation of Kyrgyzstan. Ulan had been a famous journalist in his home country, but he was forced to flee after some political and social unrest. In one men's conference I gave a prophetic word of encouragement to Ulan, reminding him that God would one day use him to reach his nation for Christ.

Fast-forward several years, and Ulan is now busy establishing radio stations all over Central Asia. God is using him and his wife, Asil, to encourage the fledgling churches in that region. I have been to Kyrgyzstan two times with Ulan and Asil while my other Russian-speaking friends accompanied us and served as translators and prayer counselors. We have seen dramatic transformation of communities all because Ulan was brave enough to take the gospel back to his country.

All this happened as the result of my friendship with Alex Novik. I had no idea that so much spiritual fruit would come from that one connection. I certainly didn't know it would affect a nation on the other side of the world.

I have yet to see the full impact of these connections with my Russian-speaking friends. God takes small seeds and grows them into huge trees. He multiplies the power of our tiny efforts. Like the drop of a single rock in a pond, the Lord creates a lasting ripple effect that can be felt for generations. He can do the same for you. Invite the Holy Spirit to use you as an influencer.

LET'S **PRAY** ABOUT IT

Lord, I want to influence those around me for Your kingdom. Take what You have invested in me and multiply it. Let me sow seeds that will grow. Show me the people You want me to disciple, and help them to disciple others after I have invested in them. Let my life be a glorious chain reaction of Your amazing grace. Amen.

ONE **FINAL** THOUGHT

If we had to preach to thousands year after year, and never rescued but one soul, that one soul would be a full reward for all our labor, for a soul is of countless price.[10]

—British Preacher Charles Spurgeon

DISCIPLESHIP TIP
You Need God's Supernatural Love

The apostle Paul loved people passionately. More than forty times in his letters he refers to his disciples as "beloved." He called Timothy his "beloved and faithful child" (1 Cor. 4:17); he described Epaphras as a "beloved fellow bond-servant" (Col. 1:7); and he called Onesimus a "faithful and beloved brother" (Col. 4:9). The Greek word for *beloved*, *agapētos*, means "esteemed, dear, or favorite."[1]

But how could more than one person be Paul's "favorite"? This wouldn't normally be possible. But when God's supernatural love flows through you, you can love all your disciples as if they are your favorites. After all, God loves all of us as His beloved children. God's fervent love will stretch your heart and give you added capacity to demonstrate warm affection, sincere compassion, and deep concern. This is the secret to effective mentoring. Love your disciples until they become "beloved" to you.

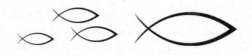

CHAPTER 3

Whatever Happened to Close Relationships?

O N VALENTINE'S DAY in 2018 a troubled young man named Nikolas Cruz used an AR-15 rifle to kill seventeen people at his high school in Parkland, Florida. We were all shocked by the news, but we weren't surprised to hear how acquaintances described the nineteen-year-old killer.[2] He was called a "loner."[3] We see a pattern here:

- Journalists used a similar term to describe Dylann Roof, the twenty-one-year-old white man who killed nine people in the 2015 Charleston church massacre. His relatives described him as a "painfully shy loner."[4]

- A former classmate described twenty-nine-year-old Omar Mateen as "socially awkward" and said "no one liked him."[5] This was after the Afghani man killed forty-nine people and wounded fifty-three in the Pulse nightclub shooting in Orlando, Florida, in 2016.[6] He was reportedly seen sitting alone several times at the Pulse nightclub before the date of the massacre. Again, a loner.

- Stephen Paddock, the gambler who fired eleven hundred bullets from his Las Vegas hotel room into a crowd of twenty-two thousand music fans on October 1, 2017, killing fifty-eight people and wounding more than eight hundred, was also known as quiet and lonely.[7]

Loneliness, it seems, can be deadly.

Americans today are lonelier than ever, thanks to the breakdown of the family, media overload, long commutes, and job pressures. Our population has increased, highways are more clogged, and we are supposedly "connected" more than ever through social media, but much of our communication is virtual and superficial. Genuine conversations are becoming as rare as handwritten letters. And the loneliness grew worse during the COVID-19 pandemic, when people were forced to quarantine at home, stay away from school, and wear masks. We also resorted to meetings on the Zoom app, which added to the sense of distanced, impersonal connection.

We have more coffee shops and restaurants than ever, but many people there eat alone or sit with others who are glued to their smartphones. We have more customer service than ever, but it's often automated. We have more retail outlets than ever, but we don't talk to a salesperson—we shop online. Soon a drone (not a real human who might actually smile and say hello) will deliver our packages to our front doors. It's too early to evaluate the statistics, but I suspect many people who died during the coronavirus pandemic lost their lives because of depression caused by isolation. In many cases, loneliness was more deadly than the virus itself.

Psychologists today have been studying loneliness—and they've proved that it can also increase the risk of obesity, high blood pressure, and inflammation, which can lead to heart disease, stroke, and even cancer.[8] Science actually reveals that humans need close relationships, meaningful touch, and loving emotional support in order to thrive physically.[9]

Dr. Vivek Murthy, who was confirmed in March 2021 to serve for the second time as the surgeon general of the United States, said he believes loneliness is a profound health issue in this country.[10] Two other prominent physicians, Dr. Jacqueline Olds and Dr. Richard S. Schwartz, declared in their book *The Lonely American: Drifting Apart in the Twenty-First Century* that people who stay isolated have multiplied health problems and that loneliness is as great a health risk as smoking.[11]

I've noticed that loneliness is a problem among Christians too. Many Christ-followers have turned their faith into a solo act. It's a "me and Jesus" kind of thing. We listen to our favorite preachers online, yet we consider church attendance optional. Church dropouts ask, "Who needs people anyway?" And even those who attend church, if they are honest, will tell you that they struggle to build authentic friendships.

Contrast this attitude to the message of the Bible. Christianity is not a private religion. We are invited to gather as a community of worshippers. We are baptized into "one body" (Eph. 4:4), the church. God calls us to radical love and close connection. First Peter 1:22 says: "Since you have in obedience to the truth purified your souls for a sincere love of the brethren, fervently love one another from the heart." The word *fervently* in the Greek can also be translated "stretched."[12] The Holy Spirit wants to stretch our love so it becomes God sized.

When Jesus called His disciples, He invited them first "to be with Him" and then "to preach" (Mark 3:14). Jesus always put relationships before ministry. The New Testament makes it clear that relationships, not programs, should be our priority. But today many churches have lost this relational dynamic. We must recover it if we want to become effective disciple makers.

How I Found Real Community in Puerto Rico

In 2013 I preached for several days at Casa del Padre—The Father's House—a small but growing church in Trujillo Alto, Puerto Rico. The congregation was meeting in a simple rented facility with tile floors and folding chairs. They didn't have a worship leader yet, so a CD player provided accompaniment for the singing. The pastor, a gentle guy named Luis Roig, worked a second job as a fireman to pay his family's bills. At that time the church's office was in his garage.

Despite the simplicity of Casa del Padre, an amazing level of love overshadowed the church's lack of sophistication. When I ministered on Sunday morning, the meeting began at 10:30 a.m., yet I didn't leave the building until 5:00 p.m.—not because I preached too long but because nobody wanted to go home. After the meeting we enjoyed a lunch that lasted three hours.

You might be tempted to say: "That's just the way Puerto Ricans are. They're very relational." It's certainly true that Puerto Ricans love to party. And their food—especially the rice, beans, pork, and *mofongo* (mashed plantains)—keep people coming back for more. But the authentic fellowship I experienced in Trujillo Alto can't be trivialized as an expression of Latino culture. No, this Puerto Rican church understands a biblical secret many of us have forgotten.

The Book of Acts tells us that after the first disciples were baptized in the Holy Spirit, they were "continually devoting themselves to the apostles' teaching and to fellowship, to the breaking of bread and to prayer" (Acts 2:42). The Greek word for *fellowship*, *koinonia*, appears here for the first time in the New Testament and occurs a total of twenty times in eighteen verses.[13]

Koinonia, which can also be translated "partnership,"[14] is a supernatural grace that causes Christians to love each other deeply. It was not possible before Pentecost because it is a manifestation of the indwelling Holy Spirit. Just as *dunamis* ("power")[15]

32

enables us to heal the sick or work miracles, koinonia knits our hearts and binds us together.

Christianity is the only religion on earth that invisibly connects its followers through supernatural affection. It makes us feel like a family—and our love for each other, if it is truly from the Spirit, transcends all boundaries of race, gender, age, and class. It motivates us to pray for one another, bear one another's burdens, and lay our lives down for one another.

After the outpouring of the Spirit described in Acts 2, koinonia caused the early disciples to share their possessions unselfishly (vv. 44–45) and to share meals often (v. 46). Many people decided to become Christians when they saw this loving community (v. 47). Koinonia was an essential ingredient in the New Testament church. It is what connected Paul, Timothy, Luke, Titus, Phoebe, Silas, Priscilla, and Aquila as a team. It is what held the early churches together in the face of persecution and caused them to lay down their lives for one another.

With all our modern sophistication, we've forgotten about the essential need for genuine fellowship. We've tried to build the church without it. We've developed a sterile church model that is event driven and celebrity focused rather than warmly relational.

We build theater-style buildings where crowds listen to one guy talk. The crowds are quickly whisked out of the sanctuary to make room for the next group. Many of these people never process with anyone else what they learned, never join a small group, and never receive any form of one-on-one discipleship. And then many Christians complain that they feel lonely, even in a crowd at their own church.

Of course we need the "apostles' teaching" mentioned in Acts 2:42, but without the koinonia described in the same verse, teaching can become dry and clinical. The church is supposed to be more like a family room than a classroom. And it is certainly not a noisy, impersonal concert where you can't hear a conversation.

Because we lack relationships today, we have tried to fill the void with technology. We think if we can create a wow factor with cool video clips, 3D sermons, edgy worship bands, and smoke machines, the crowds will scream for more. I don't think so. Trendy can quickly become shallow.

We have a relationship crisis today. Pastors and Christian leaders often tell me that they don't have any friends. Close friendships are becoming rare. This is often because we were betrayed in a previous relationship, so we close our hearts and crawl into our protective shells. Many Christians have given up on church altogether—not because of doctrinal issues but because they were wounded by someone at church.

We must return to koinonia! But you can't download it, there's no app for it, and you can't fake it. (If you want a concrete example to copy, I can give you the address of the church in Puerto Rico.) We will have to scrap artificial, event-driven programs if we want to return to the relational Christianity of the Book of Acts.

Expand Your Love Capacity

I don't like goodbyes, especially on the mission field. If you know me, you know that sometimes I get emotional in airports. It was really bad when I left Singapore in 2019.

I had spent two weeks with people from nine different churches, and I invested a lot of time and energy encouraging the people—including members of Indian, Filipino, and Indonesian congregations. I poured my life into a group of young disciples: Peter, Billy, Hani, Sireesh, Chee, Chandra, Alberto, and Tim. I also reconnected with many wonderful leaders, including Sanford, Anna, Naomi, Yang, Hazeil, Brenda, Nelson, Jonathan, Joshua, and Leslie. We shared meals. We prayed together. We experienced the bond of the Holy Spirit. And we ate durian, an odd-smelling fruit that is either loved or hated all over Asia.

When it was time for me to go through the security checkpoint at the airport, some of these people came to see me off—and a few stayed until almost 2 a.m., when it was time for me to check in. I couldn't hide my tears. I gained composure after I reached my seat on the airplane. But I felt as if my heart was being ripped out of my chest.

Why do we feel such strong connections with our spiritual family? It's because Christianity, at its core, is about relationships. We are baptized not only into a personal relationship with God but also into His corporate body, the church. God calls us to follow Him with a group of spiritual companions.

Difficult goodbyes have become a normal part of my Christian experience. The apostle Paul had this dilemma too. He missed people desperately. He told the Romans, "For I long to see you" (Rom. 1:11). He told the Thessalonians, "So having great love toward you...you were dear to us" (1 Thess. 2:8, MEV). He told Timothy, "I long to see you again, for I remember your tears as we parted. And I will be filled with joy when we are together again" (2 Tim. 1:4, NLT).

Paul's gospel flowed from the heart. Our faith is based on the astounding truth that a loving God came to earth to repair our broken relationship with Him. And since then God has sent people across oceans and mountain ranges to tell others about His love. They have often had to endure painful goodbyes.

Jesus modeled this affectionate love by investing time in His disciples. He didn't float around like a guru while dispensing otherworldly wisdom. He wasn't detached or aloof. He hiked through Palestine with His friends. They got their feet dirty together, and then He washed their feet. He fished with them, ate with them, and just hung out with them. His relationship with them was not just about the task of ministry. He wanted their fellowship.

We get this backward today. We tend to value religious performance, yet we are often bankrupt when it comes to friendships. We sit together in countless meetings but never open our hearts to one another. We've created a robotic, programmatic,

clinical Christianity that counts heads but lacks the heart of New
Testament love.

I tossed out that sterile version of Christianity a long time ago.
I've learned that ministry is not about getting big crowds, filling
seats, tabulating response cards, or eliciting raucous applause.
It's not about running on the church-growth treadmill. Religion
that focuses on externals is dry and performance based. Real
Christianity is warm and affectionate.

How would you assess your current relationships? Intimate?
Professional? Distant? Cold? Do you have close friends? Do you
live out your faith in solitary confinement? Have you pulled away
from close relationships in the church because someone hurt
you? How you answer these questions will determine whether
you will be successful making disciples—because only relational
people have the capacity to invest in others.

Hopefully we all want to see a global revival of Christianity.
We want to see miracles and mass conversions. But we forget
that New Testament revival doesn't happen without New
Testament love. You cannot say you love God if you don't love
people.

British preacher Charles Spurgeon was blunt about this. He
said: "You are no lover of Christ if you do not love his children.
As soon as ever the heart is given to the master of the house it is
given to the children of the house. Love Christ and you will soon
love all that love him."[16]

I see this love manifested in some specific ways:

- Servant-hearted leadership. The apostle Paul
  and the leaders on his team did not think of
  themselves as "all that." They weren't pulpit
  stars. They didn't ride in limousines or demand
  five-star hotel rooms. Paul was even willing to
  work a job so he wouldn't be a burden to the
  Thessalonians.

  In today's churches, some pastors have

morphed into hipster CEOs who appear only
in the pulpit and on the video screen. They may
bring a powerful message, but the idea of personal impartation has become a relic of a bygone era.
In the era of the "iChurch," we don't get on the
people's level. That's too bad, because sermons
alone don't make disciples. People need a personal touch from leaders who feel deep affection
for those they are discipling.

- Selfless investment. When Paul was in prison,
  he didn't throw a pity party or feel bad for himself. He was thinking 24/7 about the people he
  had led to Christ. He desperately wanted to see
  them again. They were in his heart. He prayed
  for them constantly "that we may see your faces,
  and may complete what is lacking in your faith"
  (1 Thess. 3:10). That kind of selfless love, modeled
  by humble leaders, sets the bar high for the entire
  church.

- Slobbering affection. The word *brethren* appears
  in Paul's first epistle to the Thessalonians seventeen times. Paul understood that when we join
  the community of the redeemed, we are bonded
  together by the Holy Spirit, who lives in all of us.
  This precious spiritual bond should be treasured.
  That's why Paul wrote, "May the Lord cause you
  to increase and abound in love for one another"
  (1 Thess. 3:12). He knew the true measure of
  Christian maturity is fervent love.

Paul also told the Thessalonians, "Greet all the brethren with
a holy kiss" (1 Thess. 5:26, NKJV). Today we explain this verse

away by suggesting that kissing was a cultural tradition that doesn't apply to us. Really?

I've been in churches where people keep their polite distance, and their lack of affection is an indicator of their icy spiritual condition. Some people criticize what they call "sloppy agape" love, but I've learned that when Christians hug one another, they are also more prone to be passionate followers of Jesus. Deep affection is a clear sign of a deep love of God in people.

One of my favorite chapters in the Bible is Romans 16. Some people overlook it because it's just a list of names. Paul sends warm greetings to thirty-three people he knew in Rome. He writes of "Epaenetus, my beloved" (v. 5), "Ampliatus, my beloved in the Lord" (v. 8), and "Herodion, my kinsman" (v. 11). Paul pours out his love for these people, showing us that he cared deeply for those who served with him.

Paul was truly what we would call "a people person." He valued relationships more than anything. He carried people in his heart, he missed them, and I'm sure he wept when he prayed for them. I can't compare myself to Paul, but I feel this way about people too. When you invest in others, they live in your heart and you feel godly affection for them. Never treat people like projects. Never walk over them to reach selfish goals.

Some leaders love crowds, but they don't value individuals. We should take the time necessary to show love to every Epaenetus, Ampliatus, and Herodion in our lives. There is a direct connection between extravagant love for one another and the spirit of New Testament revival. We must rediscover this type of love if we want to be effective in discipleship.

Learn to Become a Friend

The Bible gives us the story of Jonathan and David as a model for true friendship. It is clear from the biblical record that God put Jonathan in David's life at a crucial time in his journey to the throne. If it were not for Jonathan's covenant relationship with his friend, David would never have been able to overcome the obstacles he faced during the reign of King Saul.

The same is true for all of us. You will never achieve your maximum spiritual potential without the help of those key relationships God places around you. Yet in order to benefit from these relationships you must open your heart and take the risk of being a friend.

How can you move from being isolated to developing close friendships? Proverbs 18:24 says: "A man who has friends must himself be friendly" (NKJV). You can't wait for a friend to reach out to you. Take the first step and be willing to break the stalemate. Charles Spurgeon put it this way: "Any man can selfishly desire to have a Jonathan; but he is on the right track who desires to find out a David to whom he can be a Jonathan."[17] Here are six qualities I see in Jonathan that always challenge me to be a better friend:

1. Jonathan nurtured a spiritual bond. After David killed Goliath and moved to Saul's palace, the Bible says "the soul of Jonathan was knit to the soul of David" (1 Sam. 18:1). This is the work of the Holy Spirit. All Christians should experience a sense of family connection, but there are certain friends you will feel deeply connected to because God is putting you in each other's lives for a reason. Don't resist this process. Let God knit you to people.

I've been married to my wife, Deborah, since 1984. She is my best friend. No one can replace her in terms of the level of intimacy we share. But just because I'm married doesn't mean I don't need male friends.

A study by Relationships Australia found that more men than women had no close friends outside their long-term relationships. Researchers found that men who have a strong support network of friends didn't deal with as much stress and stayed healthier physically. And a group of researchers in Spain found that loneliness can cause a 26 percent increase in risk of dementia and an even bigger risk of mild cognitive impairment.[18] We need relationships to stay healthy.

2. Jonathan showed sacrificial love. Jonathan loved David so much that he risked his life to help him fulfill his mission. Jonathan even dodged Saul's spear in his effort to help his friend. He lived in the spirit of Jesus' words about friendship: "Greater love has no one than this: to lay down one's life for one's friends" (John 15:13, NIV). The world says we should care only about our own success. But the best way to become more like Jesus is to help someone else succeed.

3. Jonathan always offered encouragement. When David was fleeing from Saul in the wilderness, Jonathan traveled to Horesh to cheer up his friend. (See 1 Samuel 23:16.) There were times in David's life when he had to encourage himself, but in this case Jonathan was God's instrument. We need each other! If you allow the Holy Spirit to speak life and hope through you, your words can propel your friends into their destinies.

4. Jonathan offered his friend protection. When Jonathan realized his father was plotting to kill David, he not only warned him of danger but also concocted a plan to deliver his friend. (See 1 Samuel 19:1–4.) Friends don't let friends get massacred in spiritual warfare. They watch each other's backs. If you see a friend making a foolish mistake or sense the enemy is targeting him, God can use you to avert a disaster. Speak the truth in love.

5. Jonathan kept his friend's pain confidential. David confided in his friend Jonathan, and in some cases he poured out his heart in frustration. At one point he said to Jonathan, "What have I done? What is my iniquity?" (1 Sam. 20:1). When I'm going through a difficult trial, I sometimes just need to vent. Thankfully, I have loyal friends who let me process my pain— and who don't run and tell others about my weakness. This is true friendship.

6. Jonathan harbored no jealousy. At one point in David's journey, Jonathan realized his friend would one day be king of Israel. The position of king was actually Jonathan's inheritance, since he was Saul's son, but he acknowledged that God had chosen David instead. So he gave David his royal robe, his armor, and his weapons. (See 1 Samuel 18:4.) Jonathan's gesture is a beautiful picture of how we are to prefer and honor one another. Jealousy destroys friendship. If we have God's love in our hearts, we will want our friends to surpass us.

If you've been hurt in previous relationships, break out of your isolation and ask God to heal your heart. Then choose to be a Jonathan to someone else.

I see friendship as a gift from God. I could never put a dollar value on the benefit I derive from the special people the Lord has put in my life. Whether it is Luis, James, Gary, Chris, Doug, Ian, Matt, Michael, Rafael, Ryan, Sam, Quentin, Grant, Chad, Steve, Lewis, Eddie, or any of my other closest friends, I feel I owe them my life because of what they have invested in me.

These men have carried my burdens, encouraged me, listened to my pain and confessions, offered advice, prayed for me, or just provided a sounding board. I am a strong leader today because of the people who walk with me—and I would be a mess without the support they provide.

Have you become a Christian loner? I remind my disciples all the time that relationships require risk. Every time you open your heart to make a new friend, you face the possibility that you will get hurt. But you can't let fear of betrayal stop you from investing in people.

Yes, people will sometimes turn away from you. Sometimes they will ambush you, lash out at you, or vanish for months or years. But if we have God's supernatural love in our hearts, we will continue to love them.

I meet many Christians who have totally slammed the door of their hearts because they got burned in past relationships. They don't realize that resentment leads to more heartache. Cutting yourself off from people is unhealthy, regardless of how you justify it. Ephesians 4:31 says, "Let all bitterness, wrath, anger, outbursts, and blasphemies, with all malice, be taken away from you" (MEV). If you are full of negativity about people, your toxic attitudes will poison you.

Decide today to be a friend. Open your heart fully to people if you want to make a difference in their lives. Becoming relational is the first step to becoming a fisher of men.

LET'S **PRAY** ABOUT IT

Lord, help me to open my heart. Stretch my love and make me a person who sincerely loves people. I repent for closing my heart for fear of getting hurt. I renounce any bitterness or resentment that has made my heart cold. Cause the flame of Your love to blaze in my heart so that everyone I meet can sense Your mercy, kindness, and overwhelming affection. Amen.

ONE **FINAL** THOUGHT

Some Christians try to go to heaven alone, in solitude; but believers are not compared to bears, or lions, or other animals that wander alone; but those who belong to Christ are sheep in this respect, that they love to get together. Sheep go in flocks, and so do God's people.[19]

–BRITISH PREACHER CHARLES SPURGEON

DISCIPLESHIP TIP
You Need Mentors and Friends

When Israel fought the Amalekites, Moses stood on a hill watching the battle. The Bible says that when Moses raised his arms, Israel would gain the advantage; but when he let his arms down, the enemy started winning. So Aaron and Hur stood beside Moses and held his arms up all day—and Israel defeated the enemy. (See Exodus 17:8–13.) I love the fact that the Bible names the men who helped Moses.

This is true teamwork. Moses couldn't do his work alone. Even though he had a powerful anointing, he needed his brothers to stand beside him. Many leaders are tempted to do everything themselves. They don't know how to delegate, or they are reluctant to ask for help. If you want to be a strong leader, don't be a loner. Who are your Aarons and Hurs? Surround yourself with mentors, advisers, and trusted friends who will lift up your arms. And when it's time to celebrate, honor the people who helped you win. You could not have done it without them!

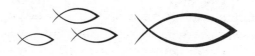

CHAPTER 4

Three Vital Relationships Every Christian Needs

I ATTENDED CHURCH WHEN I was a teenager, but at that time in my life I could best be described as spiritually clueless. I had a distant and superficial relationship with God, I was unfamiliar with the Bible, and I don't remember listening closely to any Sunday sermon. I was distracted by worldly temptations, and I would most likely have pursued my own goals and sinful desires if a young man named Barry St. Clair had not taken an interest in my spiritual growth.

When I was fifteen years old, Barry invited me to attend what he called a "discipleship group," which he was hosting at his home in suburban Atlanta on Tuesday evenings. I had no idea what discipleship was. A few of my high school friends, all tenth-graders, also planned to go.

Barry was only twenty-eight at the time, but he was already a well-known youth ministry specialist (even though he admits today that he had no clue what he was doing when he started the group). He also seemed very grown-up to me—because he was married and had an infant son. Even before I got to know him I looked up to him because he was so "old."

There were about ten young guys in the group, and we met in Barry's basement for an hour and a half each week. There was nothing fancy about the meeting when you compare it to today's modern youth ministry standards. There were no guitars or loud worship music; there were no strobe lights or smoke machines; Barry didn't use cool PowerPoint slides or movie clips to illustrate his messages. (PowerPoint would not be invented for several decades.)

We were just a group of ten average guys, sitting in a circle in a room with 1970s-style shag carpet. And Barry's wife, Carol, would always fix us a snack of potato chips and soft drinks after the session.

I don't remember the content of Barry's lessons. But I knew he was passionate for God and wanted to teach me and the other guys how to have a closer relationship with Jesus. He taught us how to have a daily prayer time. He encouraged us to read Scripture regularly. And he often mentioned that he prayed for us during his own time with God.

I had my ups and downs in those days. I struggled with doubts and fears, and my Christian commitment was weak. I didn't realize that Barry was planting the seeds of God's Word in my life in those formative years and that the Holy Spirit was working in me because of his prayers.

One of Barry's favorite phrases was "Jesus is Lord." He would say those words often, and he would write them at the close of any letter he sent me. One of the many verses Barry challenged us to memorize was Romans 10:9: "That if you confess with your mouth Jesus as Lord, and believe in your heart that God raised Him from the dead, you will be saved."

I will never forget an experience I had during the summer of 1976, just a few months before I left home for college. While I was cutting the lawn on a hot June afternoon, I saw in my imagination a road that forked into two roads. I suddenly had a vivid memory of another verse Barry had shared with us about two very different roads. Jesus said: "Enter through the narrow gate. For wide is the gate and broad is the road that leads to destruction, and many enter through it. But small is the gate and narrow the road that leads to life, and only a few find it" (Matt. 7:13–14, NIV).

I believe it was in that moment that everything Barry had ever said to me crystallized. I could suddenly feel all three years of Barry's investment weighing heavily on my soul. I could hear Barry telling me in his gentle but commanding voice, "If Jesus is not Lord of all, He is not Lord at all."

I knew that if I did not seriously acknowledge Jesus as Lord of every area of my life, I would most likely drift down the wide road of worldliness when I moved away to college. It was at that point that I firmly nailed down my decision to follow Christ faithfully. I chose the narrow path because Barry had shown me it was the best route.

When I turned eighteen the next month, Barry called and asked if he could take me to a nearby shopping mall to celebrate. He led me into a restaurant, where many of my friends from the discipleship group were waiting for us. It was all a surprise, and Barry was the instigator. Barry was not only interested in preaching to me in our small group; he wanted to have a friendship with me. He modeled for me what it means to be a good mentor.

When I got to college, everything Barry taught me began to kick in. I started having a daily quiet time each morning in my dorm. I studied my Bible daily because I knew I needed God's Word in my heart to stay strong. I got involved in a campus ministry and began discipling other students, and everything I learned from Barry guided my methods. And if I needed additional guidance, I knew I could call Barry or visit him ninety minutes away in Atlanta.

In those days I didn't refer to Barry as a mentor. I don't even know if I was familiar with that term back then. All I knew was that I looked up to Barry as a role model, and he was probably the most important person in my life. My own dad was a great provider, and he was faithful to my mother and our family, but he was distant emotionally because his own father didn't really know how to affirm him. Barry became an additional father figure for me. I wanted to be like him.

It would be many years before I fully realized how valuable Barry's investment in me was. Thankfully, even in the days before smartphones and FaceTime, Barry and I stayed close. He was in my wedding in 1984. I sat on his back porch and cried with him when his first wife, Carol, died in 1993. He prayed over me at my ordination in 2000. He traveled with me on a mission trip to China the next year. And after I began my preaching ministry, Barry and I did numerous conferences together.

Today, when Barry describes the small discipleship group he started in 1974, he remembers it differently than I do. He often apologizes, saying, "I really had no clue what I was doing." He felt inexperienced, and he refers to me and those other tenth-grade guys as "guinea pigs" in his discipleship experiment.

Maybe he was inexperienced, but I owe him the deepest gratitude for taking the risk of discipling me when he could have chosen to wait until he felt more qualified. I might have gone down the wide road to destruction if he had not obeyed the promptings of the Holy Spirit. The moral of this story is: Don't wait until you are fully equipped to make a difference in someone's life. Start now!

You Need People—and People Need You

Today I realize how blessed I am to have had—and continue to have—a man like Barry St. Clair in my life. During my travels around the world I have realized that many people never receive training from a person who maps out the Christian journey for them. Most pastors tell me they attended what they called "the school of hard knocks"—they were basically thrown into the deep end of the pool and expected to swim. Training was rare; personal mentoring was nonexistent. They never got any individualized instruction, so they don't realize how important it is to provide that instruction for others.

My job is to wave a big red flag and tell everybody who will listen that we must change our old habits. Relational discipleship isn't optional. We cannot achieve the results of New Testament Christianity if we don't use the New Testament's model of ministry. And the New Testament shows us that God uses relationships to develop Christian maturity.

When Jesus began His ministry, He didn't rent a coliseum for an evangelistic campaign, start a mailing list, or put billboards all over Jerusalem announcing His healing ministry. He did not hire a plane and drag a big sign across the sky that says, "God loves you." No, the first thing He did was assemble a group of close followers. He called them His friends.

Mark 3:14 says Jesus appointed the Twelve "so that they would be with Him and that He could send them out to preach." Notice that He was not just calling followers to perform a task. He was not a foreman employing hired hands. He wanted their fellowship first—and then He would release them to preach out of what they learned from Him.

Jesus is all about relationships. And He specifically told His disciples that He didn't want His relationship with them to be performance based. He said: "No longer do I call you slaves... but I have called you friends, for all things I have heard from My Father I have made known to you" (John 15:15). In many parts of the church we've forgotten about the essential need for fellowship and tried to build the church without it. We have developed a sterile church model that is event driven rather than genuinely relational.

We build theater-style buildings where crowds listen to one guy talk. The crowds are quickly whisked out of the sanctuary to make room for the next group. Sometimes there are so many people in the church that people need binoculars to see the preacher! Many of these people never process with anyone else what they learned, never join a small group, and never receive any form of one-on-one discipleship.

We have become so familiar with this spectator mindset that we think it's normal. Because we lack relationships today, we try to fill the void with technology. We think if we can create a wow factor with cool sermons and edgy worship bands, the crowds will scream for more. The problem is that if you build your church on what is cool and trendy, those trends will get old quickly. Then the crowd will go looking for a cooler church with trendier trends.

I've had enough of this endless pursuit of cool. I've learned that ministry is not about running on the church-growth treadmill. Religion that focuses on externals cannot produce life. If our faith does not flow out of relationship with God and result in deep relationships with others, it is a poor imitation of the type of church we see in the Book of Acts.

God doesn't want us to live in isolation. I realized many years ago that I desperately need people in my life in order to fulfill my purpose. My parents invested in me, and so did teachers, coaches, employers, pastors, role models, and good friends. I am not self-made, and neither are you. Any success we have achieved is the result of someone's taking time to instruct, encourage, or correct us.

Do you need to go deeper in your relationships? I tell Christians all over the world that they need three kinds of relationships in their lives, apart from family relationships:

1. **Pauls are spiritual fathers and mothers you trust.** All of us need older, wiser Christians who can guide us, pray for us, and offer counsel. Mentors like Barry St. Clair have encouraged me when I wanted to quit and propelled me forward when I lost sight of God's promises. In the journey of faith, you do not have to feel your way in the dark. God gave Ruth a Naomi, Joshua a Moses, and Esther a Mordecai. You can ask the Lord for a mentor to help guide and coach you.

2. **Barnabases are spiritual peers who are close, bosom friends.** Everybody should know the benefit of Proverbs 18:24: "There is a friend who sticks closer than a brother." But you cannot find faithful friends without seeking to be one first. Don't wait for your Barnabas to come to you—go and find him.

Barnabases know everything about you, yet they love you

anyway. They are also willing to correct you—bluntly if necessary! They provide accountability in areas of personal temptation. They offer a listening ear and a shoulder to cry on. And they will stay up all night praying for you when you face a crisis.

3. Timothys are the younger Christians you are helping to grow. Acts 16:3 tells us that when Paul met young Timothy in Asia Minor, he "wanted this man to go with him." Why? The apostle must have seen potential in the half-Greek convert. Timothy was inexperienced, and he struggled with timidity. But after he traveled with Paul and received loving mentorship, he led the church in Ephesus. Paul later said Timothy was like a son to him and that there was no one else with his "proven worth" (Phil. 2:22).

Like Paul, we must go out and find our Timothys. We must invest in them personally. It's not about preaching to them; they want a relationship with us that is genuine. They want spiritual moms and dads who are approachable, accepting, affirming, and empowering. If we don't mentor them now, there won't be anyone running alongside us when it's time to pass our baton.

Be on the lookout for your Timothys—or Timotheas! God will put them in your path. Invest time in them. Take them under your wing. They will not be perfect, and they may come from a broken family or struggle with personal challenges. But if you look past their flaws, your love and encouragement can transform them into mature leaders who surpass you in spiritual impact.

Relational discipleship takes a lot of time and energy, but investing your life in others is one of the most fulfilling experiences in life. Once you have poured your life into another brother or sister and watched them mature in Christ, you will never settle for superficial religion again.

Find a Paul—and Be a Paul

Mentorship is a basic biblical principle. The Book of Proverbs opens with an exhortation to listen not only to parents but also to the "words of the wise" (Prov. 1:6). The message of Christ is best transmitted through the process of mentoring. But this art has been lost in today's church—partly because of family break-down and partly because our celebrity-obsessed culture values self-effort and instant results. Mentoring is too slow for most of us because we prefer the overnight sensation. God's kingdom is built through a tedious process we don't have the patience for.

Yet I believe we can reclaim biblical discipleship. In fact, I'm convinced the church is shifting radically back to God's orig-inal plan as we reject the one-man show of the past season. Everywhere I go I find people who are hungry for authentic rela-tionships that can help them become team players and mature mentors.

I've found six types of mentors who have helped me in my spiritual journey:

1. Distant mentors. British author and preacher Charles Spurgeon died in 1892, but I consider him a mentor because I read his books often. The same is true of other dead authors such as Andrew Murray, Corrie ten Boom, Watchman Nee, and A. W. Tozer. You don't have to know a person to receive instruction from them. I've never met author Henry Blackaby, but his books, especially *Experiencing God,* have influenced me profoundly. The same can be said of author Randy Alcorn, whose 2004 book *Heaven* is one of my favorites.

2. Occasional mentors. Brother Andrew, founder of the Open Doors ministry, became a hero to me after I read his book *God's Smuggler* in the 1970s. Then, in 2004, I had the privilege of inter-viewing him at his home in Holland. Some of the things he said to me that day still ring in my ears. I will never visit him again, since he is the age of my own father, but he made an eternal investment in my life.

3. Negative mentors. Not everyone you meet is a good example. I have sometimes encountered people in positions of leadership who had serious flaws. Some had prideful attitudes; others had poor people skills; a few had selfish agendas. Rather than allowing myself to become bitter or judgmental, I studied their behavior and determined to avoid doing the same things. I said to myself, "Let this be a lesson. That is *not* how to lead."

4. Reverse mentors. You can also learn from younger people. I invest in a lot of Timothys, and they love to ask me for counsel. But I sometimes flip roles and pick their brains. One of the guys I'm mentoring, Alex, is a tech geek—so I know he will have the answer when I have a question about my computer, my smartphone, or the latest app. I also get regular feedback from the guys I'm mentoring because I want to know if I'm communicating in a way that is relevant to their generation. Sometimes the best way to mentor is to ask them questions!

5. Spiritual fathers and mothers. God has used many different mentors in my life, but there are some who invested in me in a very personal way for a long span of time. As I already explained, Barry St. Clair has been a role model, counselor, and spiritual father for most of my life, and his investment in me has now been passed on to dozens of others.

Around the same time I met Barry, the Lord also connected me with a woman from my church in Atlanta named June Leverette. June was a young mother, but somehow she and her husband, Jerry, made time in their busy schedule to teach a Sunday school class and host special events for young adults. June had a special relationship with the Lord, and she spent a lot of time studying the Bible and praying.

One day she invited me to her home and shared some scriptures with me about the Holy Spirit. Her words caused me to hunger for a deeper relationship with God—and eventually because of her influence I asked Jesus to fill me with the Holy Spirit's power. After that experience I went to June and Jerry's home many times to listen to their testimonies and to ask questions about their spiritual journeys. June became like a spiritual mother to me—and that relationship lasted for more than forty years until she died in 2020.

If you don't have mentors, I urge you to find them. If you are fortunate enough to have been mentored, then pay forward what you have received—and invest in someone else. If you want to begin a mentoring relationship, get familiar with God's pattern for discipleship in the Bible.

Here are ten qualities to look for in a healthy mentor:

1. Healthy mentors have mentors. The greatest leaders I know talk often about the people who helped them grow as Christians. No mature leader is self-made. Even the apostle Paul had Ananias to disciple him when he first came to faith. If a mentor claims he or she "learned everything directly from God," you can be sure they have a spirit of pride. Never trust a loner.

2. Healthy mentors are accessible. Some mentors keep an arm's-length distance from people, and they make you wait until the planets align to schedule an appointment. That is not the Jesus way. The apostle Paul told the Christians in Rome: "For I long to see you, that I may impart some spiritual gift to you" (Rom. 1:11). Don't play hard to get. If you are called to help other disciples grow, give them your phone number, answer their texts, and open your heart as well as your office door.

3. Healthy mentors don't just talk—they listen. Jesus is the source of all wisdom, yet when He was with His disciples, He didn't just lecture them. He often asked them questions and listened to their answers. (See Mark 8:27–30.) God gave us one mouth and two ears—so we should listen twice as much as we talk. Good mentors know how to use their ears to show that they care.

4. Healthy mentors are patient and understanding. If you are called to be a mentor, you must realize that people don't always take your advice the first time you offer it. Young Christians will make huge mistakes, ignore your counsel, and frustrate you so much that you'll be tempted to get angry, pull out your hair (or theirs), and give up on them. Make sure to be there for them when they stumble—and cry with them when necessary.

5. Healthy mentors have the courage to confront. The apostle Paul told the Thessalonians that he cared for them "as a nursing mother tenderly cares for her own children" (1 Thess.

2:7). But he also sternly warned his followers to avoid sin. Don't compromise biblical standards to show compassion. Love is kind, but it is never soft. Sometimes the most loving thing you can do is rebuke a person who is acting foolishly.

Walter Henrichsen said wisely: "Confrontation is one of the highest expressions of love. When done in love and compassion, confrontation is one of the kindest things you can do for another person. A refusal to confront when needed, is one of the most selfish things you can do."[1]

6. Healthy mentors are committed to confidentiality. When your disciple bares his soul to you, don't gasp or act shocked. Cover his sins with the blood of Jesus, and never tell others what he said. First Peter 4:8 says: "Love covers a multitude of sins." You are betraying your disciple if you tell others about his private confession. Unless he confesses to child sexual abuse or murder (which you are required by law to report to the police) his confession is between you and him. Give your disciple a safe place to heal.

7. Healthy mentors live what they preach. Anybody can post their sermons on YouTube and attract a huge audience. But sermons alone don't make a man or woman of God. Don't be duped into following people just because of pulpit charm or online popularity. What you need in a mentor is tested character, not the wow factor. And true character is not formed in the spotlight but in the darkness of life's trials.

8. Healthy mentors focus on a few. We are all tempted to measure success by numbers. But good mentors, even if they preach to huge crowds, invest most of their time in helping a small number of disciples reach maturity.

9. Healthy mentors are always growing spiritually. Jesus said a good steward in His kingdom "brings out of his treasure things new and old" (Matt. 13:52). Mentors aren't effective if they teach only what they learned forty years ago. They must stay current. Good mentors are always reading books, learning new things, and applying old truths to new challenges so they can train a new generation.

10. Healthy mentors know their limits. Jesus was the Son of God, but He got tired because He was also fully human. When the crowds drained His energy, He "would often slip away to the wilderness to pray" (Luke 5:16). Good mentors know when their tanks are empty—and they withdraw from people to get refilled. Don't make the mistake of seeing yourself as a messiah. You can give people only what God gives you. Learn to rest, pray, play, and recharge.

If you need a mentor, look for a healthy one. And if you are a mature believer, make it your goal to impart what you've learned from Jesus to a whole new generation of Christians who need healthy role models.

You Need "Barnabas" Friends

I face serious struggles regularly. I fight anxiety, discouragement, fear, inferiority, temptation, and frustration. In fact, sometimes I want to quit because of the stress of ministry! No one is immune to human weakness. But I always bring my problems to God first because the Bible says: "Cast all your anxiety on Him because He cares for you" (1 Pet. 5:7, NIV). Prayer is always my first step when I face a challenge.

Yet I also seek support from my close friends. Christianity is a team sport. Don't be so proud that you can't ask for help when you are hurting. When Moses' faith wavered, Aaron and Hur held up his arms (Exod. 17:10–12). When David felt scared, Jonathan encouraged him (1 Sam. 23:15–16). Even the apostle Paul needed friends. He said Aristarchus, Mark, and Justus "proved to be an encouragement to me" (Col. 4:10–11). Don't suffer alone. You were created for community, not isolation. Embrace the people God has sent to help you grow.

After my father died in 2018, I dreaded Father's Day because it made me sad. I honestly felt like crawling in a hole. But instead of stuffing my pain, I reached out to some of my closest friends and asked them to send me an encouraging text or video to cheer me up.

You may think that sounds like a selfish request, but my friends didn't see it that way. The texts began bombarding my phone on that Sunday morning, and they came throughout the day. I saved every message, and I still read them to this day. The words of my friends lifted me out of a dark pit.

I have learned to draw strength from my closest peers. I'm not afraid to text one of them to ask for prayer. They always text back and ask questions or call to chat. They know I will do the same for them when they are in need. But how do you find the kind of quality friend who will lay down his life for you? I have learned to watch and see who God is connecting me with.

If you want to make friends effectively, you must be willing to be a friend first. Proverbs 18:24 says, "A man who has friends must show himself friendly" (MEV). Don't wait for a friend to reach out to you. Take the first step and be willing to break the stalemate. Charles Spurgeon put it this way: "Any man can selfishly desire to have a Jonathan, but he is on the right track who desires to find out a David to whom he can be a Jonathan."[2]

After David killed Goliath and moved to Saul's palace, the Bible says "the soul of Jonathan was knit to the soul of David" (1 Sam. 18:1). This is the work of the Holy Spirit. All Christians should experience a sense of family connection, but there are certain friends you will feel deeply connected to because God is putting you in each other's lives for a reason. Let God knit you to people.

About twenty years ago, a leader of an international mission organization in Alabama contacted me at the company where I worked as the editor of a Christian magazine. His name was James. He was shocked that I answered his email because he assumed I would ask an assistant to answer his question. James and I began to have many conversations about the challenges his ministry was facing in the various countries where his mission teams worked.

Our long-distance friendship grew. Over the course of two or three years we talked once or twice a month, and I began to ask James about his personal life. He couldn't believe that I actually wanted to get to know him as a friend. For too long, people had simply used James to get what they wanted—whether it was a ministry platform, financial support, or free advice. James struggled to open his heart because so many Christians had hurt him. He wasn't sure if he could trust me, but eventually he stopped holding back.

James opened his heart and shared some of his deepest personal struggles. He had never been able to be as open with other friends. We had some long phone conversations, but eventually we met in person to discuss some painful experiences from his past. James shared things with me that he had never told another human soul. He received indescribable healing as a result. It was as if a hundred-pound weight fell off his shoulders.

When I asked James recently what happened to him during those sessions of vulnerability, he said: "The things I struggled with for many years were exposed, and the lies I believed about my worthlessness were undone. I began to heal in ways I never imagined possible."

By the time I met James in person he was already age fifty-one and totally burned out. He had no hope of continuing in ministry. But having a close friend gave James a reason to look forward to each day—and opened up a path forward. Says James: "Having a trusted friend who would listen to me, speak truth to me, hold me accountable, encourage me, and laugh with me brought me back from the edge of walking away from everything I knew. Today I am whole. Because Lee taught me how to be a friend, I have learned how to give that away to others around me. And I have an abundance of friends now."

James is now one of my closest buddies, and he offers the same kind of counsel and support I gave him in the beginning.

In fact, he became a professional life coach and helps countless people excel in their careers. I am also a better man because I know James—I can't count how many times he has prayed with me or coached me through challenges. You too will be a much better person when you allow close friends to get past your tough exterior so they can help you.

Where Are Your Timothys?

More than 150 years ago Charles Spurgeon wrote, "The Church of the living God needs young blood in its veins! Our strength for holding the faith may lie in experienced saints, but our zeal for propagating it must be found in the young!"[3] That means we can't allow generation gaps in ministry; the young and the old must work together to reach the world for Jesus. This is why mentoring the next generation is so crucial.

We often think of mentoring as a top-down arrangement. We think discipleship is basically saying: "Listen to me, watch me, and do what I do." To make matters worse, some leaders who are bossy, self-absorbed, or heavy-handed end up hurting those they mentor. Or they view mentoring as a way to get cheap labor—by forcing their mentees to serve as bodyguards, butlers, nannies, or glorified valets.

We should scrap that horribly flawed model and recognize that Jesus calls mentors to serve their disciples. If we take a humbler approach to mentorship, we might actually learn something from younger people while we model Christlike character and teach valuable skills.

The apostle Paul learned this lesson. Early in his ministry he and his colleague Barnabas parted ways because Paul didn't want to travel with John, called Mark. (See Acts 15:36–39.) Paul was upset that Mark had abandoned his missionary team. So he wrote Mark off.

Thankfully this strategic relationship was restored. Many missionary journeys later, Paul wrote to Timothy: "Pick up Mark and bring him with you, for he is useful to me for service"

(2 Tim. 4:11). Mark was quite useful because he wrote the Gospel of Mark, which he based on Peter's oral testimony.

I believe Paul had a paradigm shift about discipleship as he matured. In his early years he didn't have any use for Mark and didn't want to waste his time training a young man who had dropped the ball. Later, Paul realized that Mark had spiritual gifts that the church needed. And Paul describes Mark as his "fellow worker" in Philemon 24.

Many young Christians today are like Mark. They have a message burning in their hearts and sense a spiritual calling. But they lack training and may struggle with being consistent. They also may need healing to overcome internal struggles.

In Mark's case, Barnabas took him under his wing and nurtured him back to health. As a result of that mentoring—and Peter's fatherly influence—Mark became a spiritual giant. (See 1 Peter 5:13.)

The same will happen today when we invest in the Marks and Timothys of our generation. The greatest blessing will come when we stop looking at them simply as cogs in our Sunday morning agendas and instead recognize that the Holy Spirit is working powerfully in them—and giving them creative ideas about how to do ministry in a more relevant and effective way.

I take my Timothys on missionary trips, to speaking engagements, and to discipleship retreats I lead. But I'm learning that mentorship does not work in just one direction. Even though I'm the "old guy," I benefit in amazing ways from the time I spend with younger Christians.

- My friend Daniel Weeks is a young pastor in North Carolina, a gifted preacher, and a fitness buff. When I decided to get serious about exercise, he set me up with an easy-to-follow weight-training and cardio schedule as well as gave me commonsense advice on diet.

- My buddy David Bakthakumar, from India, is on fire for God. He works at a Bible college in Florida, and he is also an expert on computers and other technology. He helped me order the equipment I needed to upgrade my video recordings. I am technologically challenged, so having David in my life is a blessing! (Hint: churches could upgrade their effectiveness by inviting tech-savvy twenty-somethings to staff meetings.)

- Dario Perez is an immigrant from Mexico who has lived in the United States since he was a boy. When he reached out to me for mentoring several years ago, I listened for a few hours to his story. Dario is a strong Christian and a worship leader. I thought I understood the plight of immigrants before I met him, but his experiences opened my eyes to many aspects of this hot-button topic I was not familiar with. Since Dario shared the pain he has gone through, I have not looked at immigrants the way I once did. He has been my window into another culture.

- I have many friends who are millennials, or part of Generation Z, who don't always agree with me about every social issue. But I've learned a lot from them about cultural sensitivity. They are painfully aware that the American church has turned off many people by being religious, racist, sexist, political, or mean-spirited—and they aren't afraid to sound off when they think I'm being unnecessarily offensive. Their critiques have made me a better listener and, hopefully, a better communicator. I've learned to value the voices of the younger generation.

My Timothys don't drain me. They don't just take from me; they give back. When the apostle Paul thought about his disciples in Thessalonica, he overflowed with thanksgiving: "For who is our hope or joy or crown of exultation? Is it not even you, in the presence of our Lord Jesus at His coming? For you are our glory and joy" (1 Thess. 2:19–20).

Paul cherished his disciples. They were his supreme joy. They represented the fruit of years of personal investment. This is how I feel about the many young leaders I have invested in over the years, such as Mike, Omar, Joseph, Atu, Angel, Peter, Rodolfo, Helgi, Sireesh, Hakon, Alvin, Igor, and Esdras. Helping them grow spiritually is an honor, not a burden.

One of the most beautiful pictures of mentoring is found in Paul's first letter to the Corinthians, in which Paul brags about his disciple Timothy. He says:

> For this reason I have sent to you Timothy, who is my beloved and faithful child in the Lord, and he will remind you of my ways which are in Christ, just as I teach everywhere in every church.
>
> —1 CORINTHIANS 4:17

Not only does Paul affectionately refer to Timothy as his beloved child, but he also says that his disciple fully and completely represents Paul's heart, message, and values. Timothy learned from Paul so well that he became like a younger version of the apostle. He could speak for Paul because he acted like Paul—and ultimately this meant Timothy acted like Jesus. He had been discipled well, and he could be counted on to lead well. The type of experience Paul had is what makes biblical discipleship so exciting.

Your goal as a mentor is to get under your disciples and push them higher. Let your ceiling become their floor. Give them everything you have and more. Encourage them to go farther than you ever did.

Don't be intimidated if they lead better than you do, preach better sermons, or have more influence. Never compete with your disciples. Serve them selflessly, knowing that God will reward you for all the seeds you have sown in their lives. Never hold them back. Propel them forward. Shoot them like arrows so they can make a bigger impact than you ever could.

LET'S **PRAY** ABOUT IT

Lord, forgive me for thinking I can handle the challenges of the Christian life on my own. I know You want to bring special people into my life to help me grow. Send the Pauls and Barnabases who can encourage and equip me. I need both mentors and close friends to support me. And then allow me to be a Paul to the Timothys who need my influence. Amen.

ONE **FINAL** THOUGHT

If you love deeply, you're going to get hurt badly. But it's still worth it.[4]

–C. S. LEWIS, APOLOGIST AND AUTHOR, *MERE CHRISTIANITY*

DISCIPLESHIP TIP
Teach Your Disciples to Treasure God's Word

Twenty years ago I met some Christians in China who had only some handwritten pages of the New Testament. They treasured those worn sheets of paper as if they were pieces of expensive jewelry. Many Chinese believers are in prison today for printing or distributing Bibles. Are you grateful for your Bible? If you are thankful for it, you will not let it collect dust. You will study it and treasure it. You will read it so often that its words become inscribed on your heart.

I love Peter's first epistle. I've read it hundreds of times, but it is never boring to me. I see something new each time I dig deeper in those five chapters. I feel as if Peter is a personal friend because I've studied his words carefully. Recently I noticed that Peter uses the word *suffer* six times in his letter. Then I remembered that Peter was crucified in Rome not long after he wrote his epistles. Almost all New Testament disciples died as martyrs. I hope you will remember the price our spiritual ancestors paid so we could have the Bible. Teach your disciples to value God's Word as they would gold!

CHAPTER 5

You Are Called to Reproduce

MY WIFE AND I have four grown daughters. The youngest of them is twenty-nine. At our age, we aren't planning to have any more babies. Our girls are the joy of our lives—and we love it when they visit our empty nest. We especially enjoy keeping the grandkids for a weekend. But if I'm honest, I'll admit I'm glad I don't have to buy diapers anymore, drive children to school, or deal with difficult bedtimes!

Even though we're finished with the task of bringing Grady children into the world, I'm not finished reproducing. I believe every Christian is called to bear spiritual children. Jesus called us to "make disciples" (Matt. 28:19), and this is what He was referring to when He told His followers: "My Father is glorified by this, that you bear much fruit" (John 15:8).

So for the past several years I've invested most of my waking hours in discipling younger Christians. I offer them counsel and share the life lessons I've learned in ministry. We meet for coffee or meals and take trips together; we also chat using every medium available—phone, text, WhatsApp, Twitter, Facebook, and Skype. I love watching young people grow spiritually.

Discipleship is not just a hobby—it's my passion. But something dramatic happened a few years ago that proved to me how serious God is about this process of spiritual multiplication.

I was preaching at Berean Church in Pittsburgh on a Sunday

morning in October 2017. After my message I invited people to the altar who wanted to be filled with the Holy Spirit. I also had a word of knowledge that there was a young man in the audience who had an addiction to pornography.

Many people responded, but I noticed a tall guy in the middle of the group at the altar. I laid hands on his head and prayed then moved on to pray for the others. When I looked back I saw that the young man was on the floor. He was trembling and speaking in tongues.

When I finished praying for everyone, Pastor Mark Moder closed the service. But this young guy was still on the floor and still shaking. I sat down next to him and prayed quietly. I could tell the Holy Spirit was doing some deep work in him. He must have stayed horizontal for more than twenty minutes.

When he finally sat up and gained composure, I asked him a few questions. He told me he was twenty years old. He told me he came to the altar because he'd been a slave to pornography. He said it was his first visit to Berean Church.

"What's your name?" I asked.

"Dante Lee Grady," he replied.

"Huh? You're kidding," I said. I had never met anyone with my name.

"No, seriously," he said with a big smile. "I was surprised to find out the preacher this morning has my name!"

Since that day, Dante Lee Grady and I have become very close. A few months later he came to my home in Georgia for a discipleship retreat with twelve other young men. He then traveled with me when I preached at another church in Pennsylvania; since then he has gone with me on numerous other mission trips. One day he hopes to go with me to Africa.

Dante is on fire for God now. He's ravenously reading the study Bible I gave him, he's plugged in to Berean Church, and he was installed as the youth leader in 2020. He also has thousands of followers on Twitter, and he uses that platform to boldly share the gospel with non-Christians.

I never had a biological son—only daughters. But now I have a spiritual son who actually bears my name.

When I asked God about this unusual experience, I sensed that my encounter with Dante was a prophetic sign—not just for me but also for the body of Christ. God is reminding us that we must take the command to make disciples seriously. Our priorities must shift.

We've all read the research about the younger generation in the United States. Statistics show that many young adults have left the church or have no interest in Christianity.[1] Yet I've also seen that when I offer to be a mentor or spiritual father to young people between the ages of eighteen and thirty-four, they are eager to latch on.

When I offer love and encouragement to these young adults, they can't get enough. This generation isn't interested in dry religious programs, but they crave an authentic and relational connection with a mature Christian who is willing to spend time with them.

The spiritual sons and daughters I'm investing in today love worship, they want to experience the Holy Spirit's power, and they are eager to share their faith everywhere. Watching Dante become a mature follower of Christ has given me great hope for the future. It reminds me that every Elijah should have a young Elisha following him and begging for a double portion of the Holy Spirit. And if you read that story in the Bible, you learn that Elisha surpassed his mentor. (See 2 Kings 2:1–15.) That is my heart's cry—that those I invest in will do greater things than I do.

Discipling is truly the greatest adventure of the Christian life. Don't let the life of Jesus end with you—pass it on to the next generation. Be a multiplier. God wants you to reproduce His life in others.

The Process of Spiritual Growth

Our four daughters are adults now, but they lived under my roof for eighteen years, and my wife and I loved every stage of their development. But eventually they grew up, went to college, and started their own careers and families. That's how life works. It would be very strange if my adult children were still living in my house, dependent on me for money and food. The same is true for us spiritually. God designed us to become mature believers.

There is nothing more tragic than a Christian who remains like a dependent infant or a selfish, rebellious teenager. The apostle Peter wrote: "*Grow* in the grace and knowledge of our Lord Jesus Christ" (2 Pet. 3:18, emphasis added). Paul said: "We are to *grow up* in all aspects into Him" (Eph. 4:15, emphasis added). Both apostles told us, "Grow up!" That is what the process of discipleship is all about. We take young Christians under our wings, and we nurture them. Our goal is to see them blossom and bear fruit. Rather than baby them, we push them to become disciple makers. When you see them investing in others, you'll know you have raised your spiritual children well.

But even though we know every Christian is called to make disciples, many of us don't do it because we don't know how. We don't know where to start or what method to use. We have lots of books on parenting and lots of research on how children develop emotionally and physically. But we lack resources on how to take a baby Christian to spiritual adulthood.

I want to encourage you to step out in faith and start the process, even if you don't know what to expect. There are many methods of discipleship:

- You can meet with someone one-on-one for Bible study in your home.

- You can gather a small group of two or three disciples at a coffee shop to study a Christian book or a certain book of the Bible.

- Since Jesus' last recorded meal with His disciples was a breakfast, you can meet a disciple early in the morning. (See John 21:4–9.) I have done this

and found Waffle House to be a great location for
Bible study.

- You can host weekly or monthly Zoom meetings.

Or you can try one of my methods: once I gathered sixteen
young guys for an evening discipleship lesson and ordered tacos
for everyone. As mentioned in a previous chapter, I frequently
sat behind the counter at a convenience store to lead a Bible
study with one of my friends who gave his heart to Christ. I have
also conducted a three-day retreat for a group of young leaders.

In other words, discipleship is not about a particular format.
You can be creative. And it certainly doesn't have to happen in a
church. In the New Testament discipleship occurred in a chariot,
by a riverside, on a mountaintop, in homes, in jails, on ships, and
on a beach. Don't worry about where to do it. Just do it!

People often ask me whether there's a book I recommend for
discipleship. There are many good resources available. When
my friend Bill McCarthy asked me what book he should use to
mentor a younger man in New Hampshire, I said: "Bill, you are
the book." Discipleship isn't a class, and it's certainly more than
a book. You can use a book as a tool, of course, but your disciple
needs to learn from you more than he or she needs a book.

During the height of the 2020 pandemic, after I led my Indian
friend Mahipal to Jesus, I began to write a Bible study to help
new Christians grow in their faith. This study, called *Let's Go
Deeper*, provides readers with another tool to make disciples
and covers such topics as the nature of God, the character of
God, understanding the Trinity, salvation, water baptism, the
authority of God's Word, and how to overcome sin. This interac-
tive study can be used in small groups as well as by individuals,
but it is designed to help you disciple someone else. (See the ad in
the back of this book for more on *Let's Go Deeper*.)

When my mentor, Barry, discipled me many years ago, we used
a few different booklets and resources. But I don't remember most
of them. What I do remember was Barry's words and prayers. I

remember that he took an interest in me, spent time with me, prayed for me, and took me on ministry trips. He was my book.

I learned from Barry's example. He answered my questions and showed me how to be a Christian. Paul said: "Follow me as I follow Christ" (1 Cor. 11:1, MEV). Paul was an open book, and he invited his disciples to learn from his experience. Barry did the same for me. I do it for the young people I disciple. You can do it too.

I love the way author LeRoy Eims explains the process of discipleship:

> Disciples cannot be mass produced. We cannot drop people into a "program" and see disciples emerge at the end of the production line. It takes time to make disciples. It takes individual, personal attention. It takes hours of prayer for them. It takes patience and understanding to teach them how to get into the Word of God for themselves, how to feed and nourish their souls, and by the power of the Holy Spirit how to apply the word to their lives. And it takes being an example to them of all of the above.[2]

Don't make discipleship complicated. It's as easy as a conversation. You are coming alongside your mentee to advise, counsel, instruct, and encourage. When you disciple someone, you are feeding them so they can grow.

When I mentor someone I keep these eight goals in mind:

1. Your disciples need consistent time in prayer daily.

When I was a teenager my mentor, Barry, stressed the importance of having a daily devotional time with God. This has become the single most important habit in my life. You can't grow as a Christian without it. As a young man I memorized this verse: "Blessed is the man who listens to me, watching daily at my gates, waiting at my doorposts" (Prov. 8:34). God promises a blessing to those who spend time with Him.

How can you help your disciples to structure a daily quiet time? Encourage them to be realistic and take small steps. They don't have to fast forty days, read fifty chapters of the Bible at once, or pray three hours daily. It is better to be a tortoise than a hare.

If they have not been seeking the Lord regularly, they should start by reading a chapter a day and praying for fifteen minutes. First they will "taste and see that the LORD is good" (Ps. 34:8), and then they will want more. The key is for them to be consistent. When they develop daily habits of devotion, they will be surprised at how much they grow.

I know some young people who are very undisciplined. They can't go to bed at a sensible hour, they sleep too late in the morning, they can't manage their time, and they can't control their appetites or their lusts. They never developed good study habits in school either. As a result they rarely have time for daily Bible study and prayer. Sometimes they just haphazardly read the Bible on their phones or pray while driving.

But spiritual growth is impossible without discipline. Slackers will never become world changers. Just as a person cannot grow muscle without exercise and a proper diet, a believer cannot become a strong Christian without discipline. Part of your job as a mentor is to push your disciples to work hard and become disciplined so they will develop a strong prayer life and learn to make wise use of their time. Don't be afraid to set the bar high and motivate them to excel.

The Christian life is compared to a "walk" (Rom. 6:4) as well as a "race" (Heb. 12:1). Isaiah said strong believers both "walk" and "run" (Isa. 40:31). The key is to move forward. Any fitness instructor will tell you that fifteen minutes of exercise is better than no exercise at all. Yet many people assume that if they can't lift weights in a gym for an hour they won't make any progress.

The same principle applies to spiritual fitness. If your disciple can't pray for an hour, encourage them to spend fifteen minutes talking to God. Baby steps are better than no steps. They should pace themselves. They will see progress, and this will motivate them to run faster and grow stronger in Christ.

Paul told the Ephesians: "Finally, be strong in the Lord" (Eph. 6:10). I'm sure it wasn't easy to be spiritually strong in a wicked place like Ephesus. It was a dark city filled with pagan temples, demons, and sexual immorality. Yet Ephesus became a head-quarters for early Christianity.

What was their secret? How could the Ephesians be strong in a dark, sinful culture? After urging them to put on their spiritual armor, Paul told them: "With all prayer and petition pray at all times in the Spirit" (Eph. 6:18). Prayer was their ultimate source of strength. Our culture today is so much like that in Ephesus. We won't survive this battle if we aren't praying. The devil eats prayerless Christians for lunch. But fierce prayer warriors will chase the enemy away. If you teach your disciples to pray, they will grow into strong warriors.

2. Your disciples need regular Bible study.

In his first letter, John wrote to his young followers: "I have written to you, young men, because you are strong, and the word of God abides in you, and you have overcome the evil one" (1 John 2:14). If you want to make strong disciples, you must teach them to feed on God's Word. Nobody can overcome sin or become a strong Christian without a steady diet of Scripture.

If you want to build muscle you must go on a high-protein diet. In the same way, your disciples must discipline themselves to eat the meat of the Word. They can't grow just by snacking on spiritual junk food. "Studying the Word" does not mean listening to occasional sermons on YouTube. That is the spiritual equivalent of burgers and french fries. Teach your disciples to study daily, dig deep into the Bible, find the choice meat, and chew long on it. That's how they will become mature believers.

By definition, a disciple is a student. And studying is not the same as casual reading. If you want to grow to maturity, you must dig into the Word as if you were mining for gold. When I study I read a Bible passage numerous times. I ponder every word, as if I were looking at each sentence with a magnifying glass.

As a student I also write down my impressions. Then sometimes I look up the verse in my *Strong's Exhaustive Concordance of the Bible* and write down the Greek or Hebrew definitions. During this process the Holy Spirit shines His light on the Word and I receive divine revelation. Proverbs 3:13–15 says that finding wisdom from God is better than finding precious jewels. If you dig diligently in the Bible you will find priceless treasure.

Paul commanded Timothy to be a good student. He writes:

> Study and do your best to present yourself to God approved, a workman [tested by trial] who has no reason to be ashamed, accurately handling and skillfully teaching the word of truth.
>
> —2 TIMOTHY 2:15, AMP

One of the best ways to study the Bible is to read one book at a time (such as Romans or Isaiah) and slowly "chew" on each verse. The more you read a passage, the more you get out of it. The Hebrew word for *meditate* is *hāgâ*, which is used twenty-five times in the Old Testament. It can be translated "roar," "growl," "groan," "utter," "speak," "meditate," "devise," "muse," or "imagine."[3] The basic meaning is a low sound, like muttering. Church leader Dale Reeves says this reminds him of the word *ruminate*, which means to chew. When a cow chews its food noisily, the food goes into multiple stomachs. Then the cow regurgitates the cud into its mouth and chews it some more. This is really what happens when we meditate or ruminate on God's Word. We get every bit of flavor and nutrients out of it.[4]

I call Psalm 119 the "spinal column of the Bible" because it's in the center of the Scriptures. A very unusual passage, it is the longest chapter in the Bible and is divided into twenty-two stanzas based on the letters of the Hebrew alphabet.[5] The entire psalm is about the importance of God's Word. It says: "O how I love your law! It is my meditation all the day" (v. 97) and "Your word I have treasured in my heart, that I may not sin against you" (v. 11).

Why is there a special chapter in the middle of the Bible that is all about the Bible? It's not a coincidence; it shows us that the Bible must be at the very center of our lives. Scripture provides the fundamental structure of our existence.

We couldn't function without a spine. In the same way, we need the strength and stability of God's Word to be successful in life. I teach my disciples to hunger for God's Word. I tell them to make it their treasure. I tell them to study it until their Bibles fall apart—then they can get a new one. The psalmist said: "If your law had not been my delight, then I would have perished" (Ps. 119:92).

If we neglect the Bible we will be spineless, unable to make wise decisions, and weak when temptation comes. We must make God's Word the core of our lives and teach our disciples to do the same.

Paul was a master teacher of God's Word, and he was always reading. Toward the end of his life he told Timothy: "When you come bring the cloak which I left at Troas with Carpus, and the books, especially the parchments" (2 Tim. 4:13). Paul wanted his books; obviously he never stopped learning. He was a student all his life.

As a disciple maker you must be serious about your own spiritual development. English preacher Charles Spurgeon read six books a week.[6] He told young preachers: "The man who never reads will never be read; he who never quotes will never be quoted."[7] If you never read books or Bible commentaries, you are trusting your own limited knowledge.

Don't be lazy. Study hard. Don't just read the Bible—dig deep and mine its treasure. And read spiritual classics as well as current books. Reading will sharpen your blade and make you a wiser and more effective mentor. And your in-depth study will help your disciples go deeper too.

3. Your disciples must develop godly character.

God trains leaders—which is what you are raising your disciples to be—and the process can be painful. During David's long journey to becoming king, he ended up in a town called Ziklag. Scholars aren't sure exactly where this town was located, only that it was in the remote Judean wilderness. The word *Ziklag* refers to the process of shaping molten metal.[8] It was not an easy place to live.

All of us must spend time in the wilderness. When we are there we feel dry spiritually, and we may actually feel far from God. But the wilderness experience teaches us that our faith is not based on our feelings—and time in the wilderness builds character.

David wrote, "My soul thirsts for you…in a dry and weary land where there is no water" (Ps. 63:1). David didn't lose faith during times of testing. He stayed thirsty for God. He prayed constantly—knowing that he was in the forge. God was applying heat and pressure to shape him for the throne. The Lord was preparing a king. In the same way, you can't reach your maximum impact as a disciple maker and leader without spending time in Ziklag, nor can your disciples become leaders without this experience.

God shapes leaders by hand, and the shaping is a slow, tedious process. He sent Moses to the wilderness to form his character, and Moses endured years of labor, trials, and disappointments. But it was in the wilderness that Moses saw the burning bush and heard God's calling. His spiritual roots went deep in those dry times. His leadership gifts were forged in the fires of testing.

Your disciples will also have to visit this wilderness if they want to grow spiritually. Be prepared to encourage them as they trek through the dry places.

I endured seasons of hardship before every promotion in my life. I worked really hard, I felt lonely and unappreciated, and I worked for some bosses who were difficult at times. I am sure I was not always the best employee either. But in the times of pressure I learned to serve, to love, and to forgive. The fire and the pressure of Ziklag prepared me for the ministry work I do now. First Peter 5:6 says, "Humble yourselves under the mighty hand of God, that He may exalt you at the proper time." I had to embrace my dry seasons and allow God to change me before He promoted me.

We must teach our disciples how to endure the hard times. We must challenge them not to rush through the spiritual formation process. They must learn integrity, purity, humility, patience, forbearance, and endurance. They must learn to praise God during tough times. They must not avoid the fire of God's holiness or look for shortcuts. They must surrender fully to God and let Him chisel them into His disciples.

Your disciples must stand firm and wait patiently when they are in the character-building season. God's answer is coming, regardless of how we feel in the wilderness. First Peter 5:10 promises: "After you have suffered for a little while, the God of all grace…will Himself perfect, confirm, strengthen and establish you." The warfare actually makes us stronger! As a mentor you will help your disciples while they go through the stages of character building.

4. Your disciples must be filled with the Holy Spirit.

The Holy Spirit lives in us, but He does not want to just sit quietly. The Bible says the Spirit wants to manifest His power through us. The "manifestation of the Spirit" (1 Cor. 12:7) happens through the nine gifts of the Spirit listed in 1 Corinthians 12:8–10. Your disciples will begin to see these gifts operating in their lives when they are baptized in the Holy Spirit. Make sure they have the opportunity to receive prayer for this experience.

The apostle Paul warned the earliest disciples: "Now

concerning spiritual gifts, brethren, I do not want you to be unaware" (1 Cor. 12:1). But many Christians today are ignorant of the vital role spiritual gifts should play in the life of believers.

Imagine if you lived on a large piece of property your entire life and never knew there was a huge reserve of crude oil under the ground. This is the way it is for many Christians; they go through their entire lives without knowing anything about the power God has placed inside them through the Holy Spirit.

We must be filled with the Holy Spirit to experience His power. Encourage your disciples to learn everything they can about the Spirit's work. Paul said we should "desire earnestly" spiritual gifts (1 Cor. 14:1), which include healing, the word of knowledge, prophecy, tongues, discerning of spirits, and more. (See 1 Corinthians 12:8–10.) It's OK to ask God for these gifts. As your disciples pursue character and intimacy with God, ask them to pray for another level of spiritual anointing.

5. Your disciples must discover their spiritual gifts and callings.

God has a purpose for each of us. Ephesians 2:10 says: "We are His workmanship, created in Christ Jesus for good works, which God prepared beforehand so that we would walk in them." Part of your job as a mentor is to encourage your disciples to discover both their vocational callings and their spiritual callings. Young people face many questions: Should I go to college? What should I study? Should I go to ministry school? What kind of career should I pursue? Should I get married and start a family?

These are not your decisions; you certainly don't have to make these choices for your disciples. But in your mentoring role you will ask thought-provoking questions, provide resources, and pray for your disciples to discover the path that best fits their spiritual gifts, talents, interests, and special abilities. You should challenge them to surrender fully to God's calling. And most importantly, they must determine how they can eventually make disciples themselves in the unique environment in which they live and work.

Jesus desires for His followers to engage in what the Bible calls "good works" (Eph. 2:10). Good works don't save us, of course. But when a person decides to follow Christ and discovers their unique life calling, they will naturally do things to help others and show the kindness, mercy, and love of God to their communities.

When Jesus transforms a person, they may become a teacher, a police officer, a factory worker, a store manager, or an executive. But they will also find unique ways of sharing Jesus—whether it is through feeding the homeless, rehabilitating prisoners, caring for sick children, going on overseas missions projects, playing in a worship band, counseling discouraged veterans, fighting human trafficking, or other avenues of ministry.

God's love is not supposed to be stored in a bottle; it is to be channeled to others in some form of outreach. Help your disciples discover how they can shine the light of Christ to the world around them. When they give to others, they will grow.

6. Your disciples need freedom from sinful habits and emotional wounds.

The Holy Spirit is like a refiner of gold, and He works continually to make us more like Jesus. His flame purifies us from sinful habits, pride, selfishness, bitterness, and bad attitudes. The Spirit changes us daily, and the process is called sanctification. That's a big theological word that refers to the process God uses to make us holy.

Paul wrote: "He who began a good work in you will perfect it until the day of Christ Jesus" (Phil. 1:6). As a mentor you will help your disciples get free from all bondage of sin. They may tend to get discouraged if they see weaknesses or sinful tendencies in their lives. When you pray with them about these weak areas, encourage them to repent and seek healing.

When we confess our sins to Jesus, the stain of our past is totally removed. We are justified and made righteous. We are no longer guilty of our sins. Yet we struggle to believe this. That's why it's important for us to confess our sins to others. James 5:16 says, "Therefore, confess your sins to one another, and pray for one another so that you may be healed." Opening our hearts to someone else about our "junk" is very liberating.

Part of your job as a mentor is to help your disciples break free from the shame of past sins. They will at times need to confess ugly habits or embarrassing choices. Your job is to extend forgiveness and mercy. Don't judge them or act shocked. Never talk about your disciples' sins to others. Be a mentor they can trust to cover them.

7. Your disciples need deep intimacy with Jesus.

The Savior told His disciples: "No longer do I call you slaves, for the slave does not know what his master is doing; but I have called you friends, for all things that I have heard from My Father I have made known to you" (John 15:15). This is the ultimate goal of discipleship. The Lord desires for every one of His followers to know Christ in a deep and personal way. He calls us all to hear His voice and enjoy a close friendship.

When Jesus wanted to describe the Father's love, He told the parable of the prodigal son. I encourage my disciples to read Luke 15:11–32 and meditate on the character of the father in the story. The prodigal son had failed miserably. He had totally wasted his inheritance and engaged in shameful behavior. Yet the Father did not scold him, lecture him, or punish him. Instead he "felt compassion for him, and ran and embraced him and kissed him" (v. 20). Then he gave him a ring, a pair of sandals, a robe, and his old room in the family estate. (See verse 22.)

This is how God treats us. He loves us intensely. He throws His arms around us and kisses us, even though we may have squandered our inheritance and wasted our lives in sin. Our Father is happy to welcome us home. If He has forgiven our sins and overlooked our failures, we cannot keep wallowing in the shame of the past. Daddy has welcomed and restored His prodigal.

Knowing the unconditional love of God is the first step to

intimacy with Him. We will never be comfortable approaching a holy God in His throne room if we think He is unhappy with us. The Bible tells us: "Let us draw near with confidence to the throne of grace, so that we may receive mercy and find grace to help in time of need" (Heb. 4:16). Your disciple must learn to cultivate closeness to the Lord. Intimacy comes as we become more and more convinced of the acceptance our merciful Father offers us.

8. Your disciples must become disciple makers.

You will know you have brought a disciple to maturity when that person begins reproducing. Paul spent a lot of time investing in Timothy. But he told his spiritual son: "The things which you have heard from me in the presence of many witnesses, entrust these to faithful men who will be able to teach others also" (2 Tim. 2:2).

Timothy did not just receive and receive and receive from Paul; he shared what he received with others. The result was that Timothy made many disciples. It is possible that Timothy made even more disciples than Paul! This should be our goal—that the people we mentor will far outshine us.

Paul bragged on his disciple Timothy to the Philippians, suggesting that there was something special about him. He said:

> But I hope, in the Lord Jesus, to send Timothy to you shortly, so that I also may be encouraged when I learn of your condition. For I have no one else of kindred spirit who will genuinely be concerned for your welfare. For they all seek after their own interests, not those of Christ Jesus. But you know of his proven character, that he served with me in the furtherance of the gospel like a child serving his father.
>
> —PHILIPPIANS 2:19–22

Can you see the fruit of Paul's investment in this young man? Many people had disappointed Paul; some of his own disciples walked away from him or were unfaithful with their responsibilities. But Timothy showed "proven worth" (Phil. 2:22) to his mentor.

Paul mentions that he felt a "kindred spirit" (Phil. 2:20) with his spiritual son. This word in the Greek for *kindred spirit* (*iso-psychos*) means "equal in soul" or "likeminded."[9] It implies that Timothy had the same core values as his mentor. Paul had certainly done an effective job in imparting Christlike principles to him, and Timothy reflected the same strong character that Paul exhibited.

This is your challenge. Before you leave this earth for heaven, deposit your faith in young Timothys who will follow behind you. They will further the gospel long after you are gone.

LET'S **PRAY** ABOUT IT

Lord, help me to grow up spiritually. I want to produce much fruit. I don't want to stay a spiritual baby. Feed me the meat of Your Word, and help me to mature so that I can teach others how to walk with Christ. Help me grow, Lord, and then allow me to be a disciple maker. Help me to lead others to full maturity so they too can make disciples. Amen.

ONE **FINAL** THOUGHT

Our first and foremost responsibility as Christians is to maintain a strong, day-by-day abiding fellowship with the Lord Jesus by feeding on His Word.[10]

–LeRoy Eims, Author, *The Lost Art of Disciple-Making*

DISCIPLESHIP TIP
Good Mentors Are Humble Mentors

Never mentor someone from a position of superiority. The fact that you are older or wiser doesn't mean you are above them. When I disciple someone, even the youngest new believer, I never look down on them or treat them like minions. They can refresh me too. I save encouraging texts, cards, and letters that my disciples send me.

Paul told the Roman believers: "For I long to see you so that I may impart some spiritual gift to you, that you may be established; that is, that I may be encouraged together with you while among you, each of us by the other's faith" (Rom. 1:11-12). Can you sense the humility behind this statement? Paul was a spiritual father and theological genius, yet he said he richly benefitted from his relationship with his mentees. You need this level of humility. There is no room for ego in ministry. Take the posture of Jesus, wash your disciples' feet, and expect to receive from them as you pour into them.

CHAPTER 6

The Four Roles of a
Disciple Maker

BACK IN 2010 I went to the nation of Colombia for the first time to preach at a conference sponsored by two churches in the city of Barranquilla. I could have gone alone, but I asked Jason, a young pastor from South Carolina, to accompany me on the ten-day trip.

I had met Jason earlier that year at a meeting of ministers. He stood in the back of the auditorium during most of the event, and he looked like a whipped puppy. I found out that he had stepped down from his ministry position because of some mistakes he had made. He was feeling rejected and disqualified. But when I looked at Jason I didn't see his failures—I saw a huge bundle of spiritual potential. He needed encouragement, not condemnation.

When I first invited him to accompany me on my South America trip he looked at me in disbelief. He didn't expect to get another chance from anyone. He expected me to write him off. But I'm painfully aware of how many times God has given me a second chance. When we boarded our flight a few weeks later, I said to Jason: "You are going to grow two feet during this adventure." He told me the day we returned to the United States: "I think I grew two and a half feet."

Jason said this because I gave him an opportunity to try his wings at a time when he felt like a total failure. On one of the last days of the trip, a church asked if I could speak at a youth meeting. The event was not on my schedule, and I already had another event at the same time. So I recommended that they invite Jason to speak to the teenagers.

When I told Jason about the opportunity he was shocked. He had never spoken with the aid of a translator, he was in a strange culture, and he didn't expect to do anything on the trip except support me. But I challenged his mindset. "Jason," I said, "you aren't here to carry my bags. God has a call on your life. I know the Lord will use you in this youth meeting."

Sure enough, when I got to the home where we were staying that evening, I learned that God had moved powerfully in the youth service. Many teenagers had been touched by God, and some were filled with the Holy Spirit. They were thrilled, and Jason was ecstatic. The dark cloud of discouragement that had followed him for months had evaporated.

When we got back to the United States, some of Jason's leaders saw a big difference in him. They could tell he had been restored. They ended up asking him and his wife to pastor a small church that had been hemorrhaging members for many months. Jason and his wife, Chloe, stepped into that difficult situation, and within a few months the church began growing. Today that church has grown exponentially, and they have planted two daughter churches in the same region.

Nothing thrills me more than challenging young leaders by taking them on the mission field. I've done this in Nigeria, Ukraine, India, Peru, Bolivia, South Africa, and other places. It's not always convenient to share a bathroom or double the travel costs, but the reward comes when I see how much the experience stretches the young leaders' faith and accelerates their spiritual growth.

It's what many call the Timothy Principle, and it's found in Paul's words to his spiritual son recorded in 2 Timothy 2:2: "The things which you have heard from me in the presence of many witnesses, entrust these to faithful men who will be able to teach others also." Paul discovered long ago that the most effective way to expand the reach of the gospel was to invest deliberately and personally in younger disciples.

Although Paul preached to crowds, he always traveled with a small team. He wasn't a one-man show. He shared his life with the people on his team—and they became spiritual giants. But if we are going to become effective disciple makers, we must fully understand the job description.

Nobody gave me a list of duties when I first started making disciples more than twenty-five years ago, but I figured out what they are through experience. I have learned that disciple making involves four distinct roles:

1. Mentor

2. Coach

3. Counselor

4. Spiritual father or mother

I've referred to these as the "four hats" of disciple making. You will wear all four hats at different times when you are investing in a person—whether he or she is a new Christian or a leader in training. You must become comfortable functioning in all four roles, depending on the needs of the person you are mentoring.

The Role of a Godly Mentor

The apostle Paul told the Corinthians: "Be imitators of me, just as I also am of Christ" (1 Cor. 11:1). The Contemporary English Version of this verse reads: "You must follow my example, as I follow the example of Christ."

A lot of us feign humility when we say, "Oh, don't look at me. I am just a sinner saved by grace. You should look at Jesus." But that is not a scriptural concept. God wants people to have role models and examples. We need some people who are mature enough to say, "Look at me. I will show you the way God taught me." That's not pride; it is biblical mentoring.

What is the job description of a mentor? Obviously your task is to help your disciples grow spiritually. You will encourage them to apply spiritual disciplines. You do this not in a clinical way but by inviting them into your life. You are saying to them, "Watch me. I'll show you how to do it."

The concept of mentoring is connected to God's grand design to send Jesus to this world to save us. We could not save ourselves, so God sent His only Son to this sinful world. Jesus took upon Himself human flesh, became one of us, suffered for us, and yet showed us who the Father is. In the same way, when the Word of God takes root in a Christian, he or she becomes like Jesus.

The Holy Spirit empowers Christians so they can do the works of Jesus. And then as they become mature and experienced in faith, they are able to teach others what it means to follow Jesus. As I follow Christ and He teaches me spiritual truths and creates in me His character and holiness, I am then able to help others grow spiritually.

It is the same pattern Jesus used when training His first disciples. He essentially said to them: "Watch Me pray. Listen to My teachings. Imitate Me when I am ministering to others. Before long, you will be doing the same things I do." This is mentoring. And you must embrace the idea that you are called to mentor others because it is the responsibility of every believer.

When Jesus went to pray for Jairus' daughter, He invited Peter, James, and John to stay with Him in the room. They were watching when Jesus sent all the mourners out. (See Mark 5:35–40.) Then Jesus took the dead child's hand and said, "'Talitha kum!' (which translated means, 'Little girl, I say to you, get up!')—and she was raised to life" (v. 41).

This miracle was repeated in Acts 9 when Peter prayed

for Tabitha, a woman who had died. Peter sent everyone out of the room and said to the corpse, "Tabitha, arise." Peter copied what He had seen Jesus do, and the miracle was repeated. He was simply imitating Jesus. (See Acts 9:38–40.)

Once I identify a disciple, I make sure to lay down some ground rules. I always share with my disciple the following:

- **I will be accessible.** I share my phone number and email, and I make every effort to communicate regularly. I want my disciples to know I am there to support them.

- **I will be committed.** My goal is to help my disciples grow spiritually and to develop their ministry gifts. I do this through instruction, counseling, and coaching.

- **I will be prayerful.** I pledge to pray for my disciples, and then I add their names to my prayer list and pray for them regularly.

- **I will be confidential.** I promise never to divulge any private information about my disciples' lives to anyone. I want them to know their confessions are safe with me.

- **I will be expectant.** I always tell my disciples that I have high goals for them. I want my disciples to eventually mentor others. God's goal is for them to "bear much fruit" (John 15:8). I want them to surpass me in impact, and I expect that to happen!

When I mentor someone I try to find out what their greatest needs are so I can provide specific instruction. I may meet regularly with them for Bible study, make periodic phone calls, or just be available to talk and pray. I try to provide biblical advice in any situation that arises. I also may refer my disciple to a book, a podcast, a counselor, or a life coach—because I don't have all the answers.

Your disciples are listening to what you teach, but they are also watching your actions. Be a model of faith. Don't just talk; be an example. This is why I take people with me on ministry trips. If you don't go on the mission field, you can take your disciples wherever you are ministering to others. If you have a specific ministry in your church, invite your disciple to shadow you as you serve.

Your disciples need more than theories and doctrines—they need to see how you pray, how you treat people, and how you face trials. Let them get close. When they see how God works through you, they will let Him work through them.

The Role of a Coach

Who is the greatest coach in American history? You might think of Knute Rockne of Notre Dame; Vince Lombardi, who made the Green Bay Packers synonymous with winning; John Wooden, who garnered ten NCAA championships in men's basketball; Nick Saban, who was responsible for six national wins for the University of Alabama's football team; Pat Summitt, who garnered one thousand ninety-eight wins for the University of Tennessee's women's basketball team; or my favorite, Bear Bryant, who led Alabama's Crimson Tide to thirteen SEC championships.

One of the reasons Bryant was so famous as a coach was his positive attitude. He became famous for saying, "If a man is a quitter, I'd rather find out in practice than in a game. I ask for all a player has so I'll know later what I can expect."[1] He also said: "Winning isn't everything, but it beats anything that comes in second."[2] Bryant's winning attitude is what pushed so many athletes—and many future coaches—to greatness.

But the truth is that most coaches don't become famous like Bear Bryant or Nick Saban. Most coaches, just like great high school teachers, college professors, or military generals, are unsung heroes. Coaches see the potential in people and pull the greatness out of them. Coaches push people to success through motivation, discipline, encouragement, and reward.

If great coaches are needed in sports and on the battlefield, we need them that much more in the spiritual realm. We all need life motivation. And though a pastor can provide that motivation in a Sunday sermon, all Christians need someone to look them in the eye from time to time and say, "Get off the bench and get in the game."

When I was in college I was part of a ministry that was involved in evangelism on university campuses. One of the leaders came to my school to speak at an event in the student union, and I was tapped to introduce him to the crowd. I was timid at age twenty and had very little experience speaking in front of people. So when I got behind the microphone my knees were knocking and my voice sounded jittery. The campus ministry leader was annoyed by my insecurity. He said rather sternly from the front row: "Come on, Lee. Don't be shy! Preach with boldness!"

This man was not trying to be rude; he was simply exhorting me to be more confident. But I lost my composure because I was embarrassed. It was not my most stellar moment. I can promise you, however, that I learned an important lesson that day that has stayed with me.

That man was a tough coach, but he marked my life forever. His words stung for a moment, but the lasting impact made me a better person. I credit him as one of the reasons I have the confidence to preach to large crowds today. He helped me break free from my shyness.

Did you ever have a coach in high school or college who made you angry, and yet today you are grateful for his or her influence in your life? We love to hate tough coaches because they push us to our limits, make us run extra laps, and embarrass us in front of the team by pointing out our mistakes. But if coaches didn't push us out of our comfort zones, where would we be today?

Like it or not, sometimes we need to be reproved. A rebuke

is never fun. But Proverbs 12:1 says: "He who hates reproof is stupid." We should never be thin-skinned when a coach brings correction. So what if your feelings get hurt? You'll survive. But you can't grow without correction.

If you want to be a good mentor, you must learn to give correction too. That's never easy, but you aren't doing your disciples any favors if you baby them. Speak the truth in love, but never hold back if you need to bring a rebuke. Jesus said: "Those whom I love, I reprove and discipline" (Rev. 3:19). We must mentor as Jesus did.

Jesus certainly was an exacting coach at times. He rebuked His disciples for their lack of faith (Matt. 8:26). He pushed Peter to get out of the boat and onto the waves (Matt. 14:28–29). He pushed His followers to imagine what it would be like to feed a crowd with a few pieces of bread and fish (Matt. 14:16–20). He told His team they would win, even though He said they would be killed by their persecutors (Luke 21:16–19).

Once, when someone in the crowd told Jesus that His disciples could not cast out a demon from a boy who was mute, Jesus got annoyed. He sounded like a gruff coach when He said: "How long shall I put up with you?" (Mark 9:19). Our Coach expects us to have strong faith!

The apostle Paul was also an exacting coach. He told Archippus: "Take heed to the ministry which you have received in the Lord, that you may fulfill it" (Col. 4:17). Paul pushed Archippus to complete the task God wanted him to fulfill. Paul also rebuked the Corinthians for not being team players (1 Cor. 1:10–11). And he exhorted his disciples to discover their spiritual gifts and use them to build up the entire body of Christ (1 Cor. 12:4–7).

If you want to be an effective mentor, you will have to quit trying to be Mr. Nice Guy or Ms. Nice Gal all the time. You will have to toughen up. Sometimes we must provide pillows or handkerchiefs for our disciples; at other times we must provide stern rebukes.

My disciples want to be successful in life. They want to have good marriages, fruitful careers, strong character, and effective ministries. So there are many times when I must put on my coaching "hat" and be a motivator, offering advice on education, career choices, marriage, raising kids, and church involvement.

One of my main goals as a coach is to help my disciples discover their spiritual gifts. They can't achieve their full potential until they learn how God has equipped them. How do you know what tools are in your tool belt? The Holy Spirit has given each of us gifts, but some Christians leave them "wrapped" their entire lives. What a waste! We should "earnestly desire" spiritual gifts (1 Cor. 14:1). That means we should open them and use them!

I talk my disciples through simple exercises. To identify their gifts, for example, I encourage them to look at how God has used them in the past. Are they drawn to counseling people? Do they enjoy teaching? Has God done miracles when they prayed for others? Do they find special fulfillment working with children or teens? Do they love to bless people financially? These are obvious clues to knowing how God has wired them. I invite them to ask the Lord to show them their "sweet spot" of ministry. Then I encourage them to learn everything they can about that gift and sharpen it with training. The more they use it, the more impact they will have.

As a coach I also ask a lot of questions, such as:

- What are your natural talents (such as singing or artistic abilities)?

- What are your learned abilities (such as playing a musical instrument or speaking a foreign language)?

- What types of work or ministry activities give you the most fulfillment?

- Have you identified your spiritual gifts? (An online test at spiritualgiftstest.com can help you do that.)

- What are your biggest goals and dreams?

- How has God spoken to you—through a prophetic word, dream, vision, or during prayer—to show you His plan for your life?

Asking your disciples such questions helps them step into their callings. Besides helping my disciples discover their potential, I also try to provide the loving support they need when they are going through tough times. One of the most important things a coach can say is, "Hang in there."

I love my ministry work, but it's not easy. Part of my job involves trusting God to provide funds to pay for overseas missions projects. God has provided miraculously in the past. But sometimes it's discouraging to look at my bank account and see the numbers going down instead of up. Sometimes I feel like quitting because nothing seems to be happening after I pray.

That's when I remember 1 Timothy 6:12, which says, "Fight the good fight of faith." Paul explains here that faith is a struggle. The second occurrence of the word *fight* in this verse is the Greek word *agōn,* from which we get the word *agony.*[3] Walking by faith is not for wimps. It is intense warfare!

Gideon was a timid man who struggled with inferiority. But the angel of the Lord came to him and said: "God is with you, O mighty warrior" (Judg. 6:12, MSG). Gideon didn't believe those words. He saw himself as a failure. But eventually he became a champion. God wants to turn your disciples into mighty men and women of God also, but they must break free from old mindsets to see their true identity. They can be changed from wimps to warriors!

Part of my job as a coach is to help my disciples see who they are in Christ. Life may have programmed them to think they are failures, stupid, weak, inferior, or unlovable. Yet there are so many scriptures that tell us who we really are. The Word of God says we are "righteous," "forgiven," "clean," "accepted" by God, "victorious," and "bold." I made a list of scriptures to help my disciples understand their new identity. (This list, "Renew Your Mind With God's Word," is an appendix at the end of the book.) As we meditate on what God says about us, we will be transformed.

The Role of a Counselor

Some people are transformed overnight after they surrender their lives to Jesus. They throw their drugs out the window, apologize to the people they've wronged, break off unhealthy relationships, and make a 180-degree turnaround. I love dramatic conversions.

But the process of change is slower for most of us. While the new birth is indeed an instantaneous experience, salvation is not. We aren't just "saved" in an emotional moment at a church altar; we are "being saved" (1 Cor. 1:18) on a daily basis. Like Lazarus, who emerged from his tomb wrapped in graveclothes, we can experience the miracle of salvation and yet remain bound. Jesus told those standing near Lazarus, "Unbind him, and let him go" (John 11:44).

Most of us Christians are bound by sinful habits and shameful memories when we first begin our spiritual journey. We need someone to unwrap us.

I minister to countless Christians who struggle with various forms of brokenness. Some are addicted to behaviors or substances; others are emotionally crippled because of their upbringing; still others are haunted by childhood trauma. Often our advice to them is as insensitive as it is unrealistic. We say: "Get over it. If you're a Christian you can't struggle with those things now." Or sometimes we offer pat answers, such as, "Just read your Bible and your problems will go away." Faith does not work that way in the real world.

Christians stumble. Christians struggle. Christians wrestle with addictions. While I would love instantaneous change, the Bible speaks of both regeneration (which happens at the moment of conversion) and the "renewing by the Holy Spirit" (Titus 3:5), which is a divine process.

Jesus promised He would take us through the steps toward healing. When He began His ministry in Nazareth, He opened the scroll and read: "The Spirit of the Lord GOD is upon Me, because the LORD has anointed me to bring good news to the afflicted; He has sent me to bind up the brokenhearted, to proclaim liberty to captives and freedom to prisoners...to grant those who mourn in Zion, giving them a garland instead of ashes" (Isa. 61:1, 3).

A person can be a Christian and yet still be dragging a ball and chain behind them. They may be one who "mourns in Zion." Many believers who struggle with secret sin or emotional baggage stuff their problems under the proverbial rug and pretend to be free. But their masquerade usually doesn't end well.

When I disciple a person I take them through a process of inner cleansing, knowing that they may still feel as if they are held captive by certain spiritual strongholds. We discuss their past in a private setting, and I ask probing questions in seven key areas. (See the list that follows under the heading "Spiritual Cleansing Prayer Session.")

I ask my disciples to confess their past sins or hang-ups, and then we pray for healing and closure. I also remind them of the power of Christ's blood to set them free from sin and shame. Don't let your disciples hobble around in graveclothes. Your job is to unbind them.

The goal of the following prayer exercise is to help your disciple come clean from any issues of sin that have hindered their spiritual growth. To begin they should answer the questions I've listed as thoroughly as possible. Assure them that everything they share will be kept in confidence, and tell them that anything you write down will be given to them when you are finished. (I write down things during the prayer session so I know what to pray for, but I never keep a copy.) The questions are designed to provide background information that I will use in our prayer times.

After their confession, I go over the areas that need prayer, and then we pray together. I apply the blood of Jesus to any area that needs repentance or healing. I may also ask my disciple to repent for certain things. After we pray, I always give the sheet of paper to my disciple and invite them to destroy it however they prefer. I want them to know that Jesus does not keep a record of our sins after we confess them.

James 5:16 invites us to live an open life: "Confess your sins to one another, and pray for one another so that you will be healed." All disciples must learn to be transparent and quick to repent when they stumble. Transparency requires us to open our hearts with our close friends or with those who are mentoring us.

We must all choose to live with accountability. We must confess our sins quickly, never hide our struggles, and allow God to heal the areas of our lives we are ashamed of. People who learn to be vulnerable will become victorious.

Following is the list of sins I discuss with my disciple when I conduct this prayer exercise.

Spiritual Cleansing Prayer Session

Unforgiveness. Are you nursing a grudge? Is there anyone in your life you have refused to forgive? You'll never know the forgiveness of Jesus if you hold resentment in your heart toward others. Jesus said He can't forgive us if we can't forgive others. (See Matthew 6:15.) Bitterness is like acid. It will corrode your soul until you forgive those who hurt you. Forgive anyone from your heart if you have bitterness toward them.

Sexual sin. Many people today have engaged in sex outside marriage. And though society says this is acceptable, the psychological damage caused by fornication, abortion, homosexuality, adultery, incest, perversion, and pornography is real. The chains of sexual sin are strong, but Jesus can shatter them when we confess our sins and choose purity. Also, many people today are struggling with sexual confusion, either about their sexual orientation or their gender identity. Are you confused in any of these areas? Confess everything and receive total cleansing by the blood of Christ.

Addiction. You may have fallen into the trap of using alcohol, nicotine, illegal drugs, or prescription medicines to numb your emotional pain. Yet the Holy Spirit can go to the root of your brokenness and heal your soul. Confess any involvement in substance abuse.

Occult involvement. Participation in any form of witchcraft (séances, fortune-telling, hexes, spells, satanic covenants, or horoscopes) opens the doors of our spirits to demonic influence. Only the authority of the name of Jesus can break the spiritual chains forged by participation in witchcraft. Doors can be opened to demons also by involvement in occult organizations such as Freemasonry and association with New Age teaching, crystals, astral projection, or Hindu or Buddhist idols. These things need to be renounced verbally, and if your disciple keeps any physical objects, books, or occult paraphernalia in their home, they should get rid of them.

Abuse. A huge percentage of people today, both men and women, have experienced some form of sexual abuse—either as children or as adults. Sexual abuse brings inordinate amounts of shame and causes the victim to think they are responsible for the actions of the perpetrator. These experiences need to be shared in confidence so the victim can be assured they did not cause this damage to themselves. Then the shame can be uncovered and removed. Other forms of abuse should also be discussed, including domestic violence, verbal cruelty, bullying, and psychological abuse.

Father and/or mother wounds. Our relationship with our parents shapes our personalities and identities. Yet many people struggle because of absentee fathers, distant parents, abandonment, or parental cruelty. And some people also suffer because one or both parents were addicted to drugs or alcohol. Talking honestly about the wounds we received from parents is a key to emotional healing. Don't let your disciple hide the pain of these wounds. Encourage them to talk about them and receive the healing of Jesus.

Fear, anxiety, and depression. Everyone has natural fears. It's normal to stay away from snakes or spiders, for example. But other fears, such as those caused by traumatic life experiences, are unnatural. Many people have been devastated by poverty, natural disasters, family breakups, accidents, or war. The Holy Spirit can bring supernatural peace to your disciple's troubled mind and deliver them from the shackles of post-traumatic stress.

Other Christians have irrational anxiety. And many Christians are gripped by a powerful spirit of heaviness that is linked to rejection or disappointment. Depression can lead to self-hatred, eating disorders, sleep problems, and even suicide. Yet Jesus offers abundant life and a sustainable joy. Talking openly about these problems will release healing.

When you pray with your disciple or counsel them about their problems, keep in mind that you are not a licensed professional counselor. No one is asking you to have all the answers or to talk about topics you don't understand. Don't feel pressure to be an expert when you aren't. Many times I have had to refer my disciples to a professional—because I could not help them, their emotional problems were too severe, or there was a possibility they needed medication.

Don't feel pressured to "fix" your disciple. Only the Holy Spirit can do that! You are simply the facilitator. But you are qualified to pray for them, offer insights from Scripture, and point them to Jesus, who is the ultimate Healer.

The Role of a Spiritual Father or Mother

My daughter Margaret was "pregnant" for almost three years with her first child. No, she didn't actually carry a baby in her womb that long. But it took almost three years for her and her husband, Rick, to go through the adoption process. It was a fascinating journey for them—and for me as the grandfather who watched the miracle unfold from the sidelines.

When Margaret and Rick worked at a Christian college in

Georgia, they took a team of students to Ethiopia for an evangelistic outreach. They learned about the plight of the children of that country during their visit, and they felt God was calling them to adopt an Ethiopian baby.

The dream grew in Margaret's and Rick's hearts, and they officially launched the adoption process in January 2011. It was tedious and expensive. The wait seemed endless—sort of like standing in line at the post office for twenty-six months. Bureaucracy caused the process to move at a snail's pace—and it seemed even slower after they learned they were assigned an infant boy and got a picture of him.

I was more impatient than my daughter and son-in-law were during the course of the adoption. They held on to their dream, even when the adoption agency faced some serious problems. To keep focused, Margaret ran a marathon to raise awareness of the need for international adoption. She decided that since she didn't have to go through the pain of childbirth to have this baby, the least she could do was run twenty-six miles.

Her stamina and perseverance paid off. Eventually she and Rick traveled to Addis Ababa, Ethiopia's capital, to do the last interviews and get the final paperwork approved. They arrived there just in time to celebrate their son's first birthday. Finally they landed at the Atlanta airport with their African bundle of joy.

His first name is Grady. His middle name is Bereket, which we've been told means "blessed" in the Amharic language. He is a very fortunate child because approximately 3.1 million children in developing countries die from hunger every year, and many Ethiopian children often die of malnutrition or easily treatable childhood diseases.[4] If my grandson had stayed in his homeland in poor conditions, the odds are that he might not have survived past age five. That's why international adoption is such a vital cause and why more Christians today are responding to this need.

When Margaret was young, I used to tell her and her sisters that they could marry guys from any racial background as long as they were Christians. Margaret decided to marry Rick, a white guy from Georgia—with red hair! But eventually she and Rick brought a dark-skinned African boy into their family because they know God's love makes racial differences irrelevant.

When Margaret and Rick made their first trip to Ethiopia to begin the legal adoption process, I was struck by how far they traveled to provide this child the nurture and protection he needs. They flew sixteen thousand miles—two times—to adopt Grady. Then they spent a lot more money securing the paperwork to legalize his adoption. The entire process reminded me of how God went to great lengths to adopt me into His family.

When we dedicated Grady to Jesus at Margaret and Rick's church in South Carolina, I also adopted him in my heart as my own grandson. I don't think of him as any less a member of my family than I do my biological grandchildren. Grady belongs to our family. He is in my heart.

And this is what happens when you invest in disciples. They grow on you. The more time you spend with them, the more precious to you they become. You will eventually carry them in your heart as if they were members of your own family.

Discipleship is not just teaching or coaching people in a clinical way. It requires a 100 percent emotional investment. Paul didn't hold back when he was with his disciples. He told the Philippians: "How I long for you with all the affection of Christ Jesus" (Phil. 1:8). That's intense!

You cannot be half-hearted when you spend time with your disciples. Your heart should gush with love, sincerity, and genuine concern. Don't be fake. Don't keep your disciples at arm's length. Be an affectionate father or mother. Paul said: "I have you in my heart" (Phil. 1:7). The depth of love you show your disciples will inspire them to connect deeply with Jesus.

Father's Day isn't a happy time for many people because they had bad experiences with their dads. Many fathers are cold, harsh, distant, or abusive. Some fathers abandoned their kids. And some never showed affection or even once said, "I love you." That's why many people struggle to view God as a loving Father.

This is part of your job as a disciple maker. You can show the Father's unconditional love. Psalm 145 describes God as "gracious," "merciful," "near," "kind," "good," "slow to anger," and generous (vv. 8–9, 14–18). As a spiritual father or mother you must reflect these qualities. Pour on the encouragement. Be merciful when your disciple makes a mistake. Show affection. Be available. Tell them, "I love you like crazy!" as my second grandson often tells me. Offer your disciples firm but loving correction. And never give up on them. Your example will help them to experience the Father's love in a tangible way.

A few years ago when I was in the city of Cali, Colombia, I prayed for a guy named Luis who was abandoned by his father at a young age. His father later died. I realized he had never had a father's blessing. So I knelt in front of him, looked him in the eyes, and said, "Luis, if you were my son I'd be so proud of you." Luis began to sob, so I gave him a big father's hug. He received deep healing in that moment, all because of a few powerful words.

God gave you a mouth, and you can use it for good or bad. Some people spend all their time complaining, cursing, and abusing others—and their soul becomes bitter. But God calls us to bless, encourage, affirm, edify, and speak life.

Proverbs 10:11 says, "The mouth of the righteous is a fountain of life." When you mentor someone, let God's life flow from your mouth. Be sweet—not bitter and negative. Your job is to build up, not tear down. If your goal is always to encourage, even your firm correction will be received and appreciated.

I love the moment in Scripture when Jesus changed Simon's name. He said: "Blessed are you, Simon Barjona....I also say to you that you are Peter, and upon this rock I will build My church" (Matt. 16:17–18). Jesus saw something special in Peter. By giving him a name that means rock, He was seeing past Peter's doubts and weaknesses. He called him into his true identity as a strong apostolic leader.

Peter didn't always act like a rock. He was often unstable, and he was so concerned about his own welfare that after Jesus' arrest, he denied knowing Him. But ultimately Peter became the solid rock that Jesus said he would become. In the same way, you can speak to the destiny of those you mentor. Your job is to see their potential. Give them scriptures. Text or call them and remind them of their purpose, especially when they have failed. Your words of blessing will build them up and catapult them to a higher level of spiritual maturity.

Paul told the Corinthians: "For if you were to have countless tutors in Christ, yet you would not have many fathers, for in Christ Jesus I became your father in the gospel" (1 Cor. 4:15). There's a difference between an instructor and a father. It is good to mentor people, and it's good to preach sermons. But the best preachers don't just speak behind pulpits; they also sacrificially invest their lives in people.

Do you want to become a spiritual parent? You cannot be a father or mother if you have not been properly fathered and mothered. This process happens mainly by spending time with God and discovering His unconditional love for you. It also happens when a caring mentor invests in your life. Being loved, corrected, coached, and encouraged by a true spiritual father or mother will help you do the same for many others.

There have been times when God has given me a prophetic message, some practical advice about a problem, or just a simple word of encouragement for various friends in ministry. Sometime after I shared, my friends told me those words became significant signposts for them. They received supernatural strength from our conversation. Even years later they still treasure the words I shared.

Proverbs 10:21 says, "The lips of the righteous feed many." Don't just look for encouragement for yourself. Learn to give it. People need to be affirmed, assured of God's love, and reminded of God's promises. Let Jesus use you to inject strength and hope into those around you.

I want to encourage you in your ministry of mentoring. You are a disciple of Jesus, and you are bearing fruit. God is using you as a disciple maker. Like Abraham, you will have many spiritual children. Keep investing in the people God has placed in your life. If you continue to sow, you will reap. Don't give up. Don't let setbacks or delays discourage you. Even though you may feel weak, you are strong in Christ. The Holy Spirit is working in you and through you. Be strong in His grace, and pour His life into others.

LET'S **PRAY** ABOUT IT

*Lord, I realize that discipleship requires a huge invest-
ment. Help me to be a good mentor, coach, counselor, and spiritual father or mother to the people I'm
training. Give me the words to encourage them. Give
me the advice to help them find their life purpose. Give
me patience when my disciples stumble or fail. And
may Your Holy Spirit break all chains of bondage in
their lives. Amen.*

ONE **FINAL** THOUGHT

You teach what you know, but you reproduce what you are.[5]

—HOWARD G. HENDRICKS, LONGTIME PROFESSOR,
DALLAS THEOLOGICAL SEMINARY

DISCIPLESHIP TIP
Expect Your Disciples to Surpass You

Your job as a mentor is to invest in your disciples so they grow into mature disciple makers themselves. Titus is a great example of this in the Bible. Paul led Titus to Christ and called him his "true child" (Titus 1:4). Paul then took Titus on trips and trained him to be a leader. Eventually Paul called Titus his "partner and fellow worker" (2 Cor. 8:23).

Later we see that Paul appoints Titus to lead the church in Crete. And in Paul's last letter he says Titus has gone to the uncharted mission field of Dalmatia (2 Tim. 4:10), part of which is modern Albania. Titus became a bold apostle just like Paul! This is your challenge–nurture your disciples until they grow into everything God called them to be. Don't baby them; challenge them to full maturity. And don't keep them "below" you; expect them to do far more than you ever could!

CHAPTER 7

The Six *I*'s of Discipleship

ANY CHRISTIANS MISTAKENLY believe discipleship happens only when we attend a weeknight Bible study or Sunday morning class at a church. Certainly God can use traditional situations like that. But I am concerned that too often we make discipleship a sterile concept—cold, formal, and clinical. If I could, I would rent an airplane and fly a banner across the sky that says: "DISCIPLESHIP IS NOT A CLASS!"

Discipleship can happen anywhere—a coffee shop, a restaurant, a park, a gym, or a living room—and it happens mostly through two-way conversations, not dry lectures. I have trained disciples in the back of a gas station, on a train in India, on a hike through a forest, and through FaceTime calls. And discipleship is not just the job of a professional, salaried pastor; every born-again Christian is called to the task of making disciples. That means you and me!

Because we have not seen enough healthy models of relational discipleship, it's important for us to visualize what it really looks like. How do we make disciples, practically? For years I have used this simple, six-point list—"The Six I's of Discipleship"—to help people understand the job description of a disciple maker.

The First *I*—Identify

One of the first things Jesus did when He started His ministry was choose His closest followers. This was not a haphazard decision. Luke 6:12–13 says Jesus "spent the whole night in prayer to God" before He chose the twelve men He would train. Mark 3:13–15 describes it this way:

> And He went up on the mountain and summoned those whom He Himself wanted, and they came to Him. And He appointed twelve so that they would be with Him and that He could send them out to preach, and to have authority to cast out the demons.
>
> —MARK 3:13–15

Notice that Jesus called His disciples, first of all, "so that they would be with Him" (Mark 3:14). He called them to a *relationship*; that was His priority, even before the important task of preaching. Jesus chose twelve men—Peter, James, John, Andrew, Philip, Bartholomew, Matthew, Thomas, another James, Thaddaeus, Simon, and Judas (see vv. 16–19)—so that He could know them, invest in them, and model for them what it means to walk in close fellowship with the Father. He knew that after three and a half years they would be ready to follow in His steps.

The apostle Luke points out that Jesus didn't leave out the women. Unlike other Jewish rabbis, Jesus had women followers, and some of their names are mentioned in Luke's Gospel. The apostle writes, "The twelve were with Him, *and also* some women" (Luke 8:1–2, emphasis added). He mentions Mary Magdalene, Joanna, Susanna, and "many others," and he says these devoted women also supported Jesus' ministry financially. (See verses 2–3.) Jesus obviously was selective when He identified which women He should train.

Jesus' example shows us how important it is for us to choose the right people to mentor. We don't draw names out of a hat. We don't trust in our own good ideas. We allow God to show us the people we are supposed to disciple. This is God's work, so we must follow His leading to do it.

The apostle Paul was always looking for what I call "God connections." He met Timothy in the city of Lystra, and he befriended him and took him on his missionary journey. (See Acts 16:1–3.) Before long Timothy became Paul's spiritual son. (See 1 Timothy 1:2 and 1 Corinthians 4:17.) After Paul led Lydia to faith, she became a key player in the early church. (See Acts 16:14–15, 40.) Later Paul met a young man named Titus, and he became known as Paul's "true child in a common faith" (Titus 1:4). Titus eventually matured into a powerful leader who was the overseer of the churches of Crete.

The Holy Spirit is the one who connects us to certain people— always for His bigger purpose. You must prayerfully follow the Spirit, and He will do the connecting. But if you want to connect with people, you must have an open heart. You should be willing to pray, "God, if You want me to make disciples, bring the people You want me to mentor."

When I intentionally started making disciples, I prayed that God would bring the right people into my life. I noticed that immediately I began to meet young people from foreign countries. I wasn't going out of my way to meet foreigners; it just happened. Before long I had several young men in my life who had unusual names. I became close to Kelechi Okengwu from Nigeria, Medad Birungi from Uganda, Sireesh Kumar from India, Ricardo Quinteros from El Salvador, Rodolfo Bermudez from Mexico, Atu Munde (a Malawian living in South Africa), Almir Ishmametov from Kyrgyzstan, Susheel Saleem from Pakistan, and Kevin Senapatiratne—whose parents came to the United States from Sri Lanka. Try saying those names quickly!

I soon realized that God had a strategic reason for connecting me with young people from other nations. The Lord obviously wants to take the gospel across racial and ethnic lines. This is His divine strategy, and He included me in His divine plan.

A few years ago during a visit to Christ for the Nations Institute

(CFNI) in Dallas, the staff of the school housed me in a furnished apartment on campus. I knew I would be there for about five days, and I was speaking only a few times a day. So when I addressed the students in a morning chapel service, I mentioned that I was staying on campus and that students were welcome to drop by for an informal visit. I made myself accessible.

My close friend Michael Cole, who was a CFNI staff member at the time, was horrified. "Lee, I can't believe you told everyone where you are staying," he said. "Are you sure you want students coming by your place? Don't you want to rest?"

I laughed and told Michael I didn't come to the school to rest; I came there to serve. I welcomed small groups of students into my apartment that week because I've learned through the years that the Holy Spirit is involved in connecting me with people for the purpose of discipleship.

On Friday evening of the week I stayed at CFNI, I hosted an informal question-and-answer session with some of the guys who lived at the school. One of the young men who came to that meeting was a student from India named David Bakthakumar.

David sat quietly in the back of the room at that meeting, but I could tell he was hungry for God and spiritually perceptive—even though he was a bit shy. He asked thoughtful questions. I knew I was supposed to connect with him, so before the end of the evening we swapped phone numbers. That began a wonderful discipleship relationship.

Over the next year I counseled David as he stepped into a youth pastor position. I stayed connected with him as he took a position at a Bible college in Florida. I prayed for him during his courtship and marriage to his wife, Blessing. Today David is like a son to me. He often calls or texts me for advice. And since we met he has traveled with me on numerous ministry trips. One day we hope to travel to India together.

Whenever God has instructed me to disciple someone, I have always had a clear sense of connection with the person. You must learn to discern when the Holy Spirit is knitting your heart with another believer in this way. Ephesians 4:3 urges us to be "diligent to preserve the unity of the Spirit *in the bond of peace*" (emphasis added).

I have learned to pay attention when the Lord is linking me with someone in "the bond of the Holy Spirit." I am sure you have sensed this at times. We often talk about "clicking" with a person; you may have just met the person, yet you feel you have a lot in common and it almost seems you have known them for years. This is what I have learned to discern as a God connection.

At times someone has come to me and asked, "Would you mentor me?" But not all my disciples have been that straightforward. Others have assumed I might be too busy, but they asked, "Do you think we could spend some time together? I have a lot of questions about spiritual growth." Some of my disciples came to me and simply asked for input on a specific issue, but their query began a lifelong relationship.

In a few other cases I sensed God might be linking me to someone, so I offered my help by saying, "If you ever need to talk, I am happy to make myself available." That offer led to a long-term discipleship relationship. If you sense that someone might be looking for spiritual input, you can say something like this:

- "I'm starting a Bible study in my home on Tuesday nights. Would you like to join?"

- "Have you been looking for a way to grow spiritually? I'd love to help you."

- "I've been walking with the Lord for several years. I'd love to meet you for coffee and share more about spiritual growth if you are interested."

Each relationship I have with a disciple is special, and in every case God orchestrated our connection. I met a young Cuban named Abdiel López when he was helping me load my slides into a computer before I spoke at the Bible college he attended in

South Carolina. Within a few months Abdiel was serving with me closely as my ministry assistant. Now he is translating for me when I minister to Latin Americans, and it won't be long before he goes to those countries to preach in my place.

God is in the business of forming discipleship relationships. When I have led people to Christ for the first time, I have felt a natural obligation to remain involved in their lives and help them grow spiritually. But some young people who were already saved have had the boldness to approach me and ask for mentoring. In most cases I could sense the Lord was working to knit our hearts. Be sensitive to the Holy Spirit and He will connect you with the right people.

Never underestimate how God can transform the person you are mentoring. When Jesus told His disciples, "I will make you fishers of men," those Galileans didn't seem to have a big future ahead of them. They were going nowhere. But Jesus saw something greater. He turned them into world changers! Don't focus on your disciple's flaws. See the potential, and then unlock it and release it through love, training, and encouragement.

The Second *I*—Invest

I always tell people that "invest" is spelled T–I–M–E. Mentoring others will totally reorder your schedule. Discipleship requires a huge emotional investment. You cannot do it half-heartedly. The people I disciple are like sons and daughters to me. When you mentor someone you invest prayers, tears, texts, phone calls, and face-to-face time. Don't start a discipleship relationship unless you are willing to lay your life down for that person.

Several years ago I performed the wedding of a young couple, Steven and Brandy. Steven Semones has been like a son to me since I began mentoring him in 2010. The night before his wedding we had a very special chat at a yogurt shop near my hotel in Myrtle Beach, South Carolina.

To this day Steven reminds me of our two-hour conversation. "You told me I could ask you any question I wanted," Steven said.

"You were so transparent and honest." That place was not fancy—we were sitting on metal chairs on a sidewalk outside a TCBY yogurt shop. But it marked Steven forever.

When I spend time with a disciple I interact with them as if it will be the last time I see them. I make the most of the opportunity. I engage deeply. I make eye contact, show concern, and listen carefully. Then I prayerfully pour out encouragement and counsel.

Proverbs 25:11 says: "The right word at the right time is like a custom-made piece of jewelry" (MSG). If you let the Holy Spirit direct your words, your disciple will treasure your counsel for a lifetime. Look for those "TCBY" moments. Invest your life. A simple conversation can be an unforgettable, life-changing moment.

When I raised my four daughters I had regular "dates" with each one. I do the same now with my spiritual sons. You may have a discipleship group, but don't relate to the members only as a group. Pull each one aside. Give personal affirmation. Make them feel special.

Years ago I began the practice of sending a short text to my disciples each week. I called it my "Discipleship Tip from Lee." I could have sent it as a group text, but I know that most people don't like to get texts in that format because if they reply to it, their answer is sent to everyone. So I decided to send these texts individually. I couldn't imagine Jesus group-texting His followers! I decided to take the extra time to send each tip personally because I wanted a one-on-one relationship. Your investment in your disciple is most effective when it is the most personal.

Jesus trained many disciples, but He gave personal attention to each of them. He invited Thomas to touch His wounds after the resurrection (John 20:27). He told Nathanael He had noticed him under the fig tree (John 1:48)—and Nathanael never forgot that! He talked with Mary Magdalene privately at the tomb (John 20:14–16). Jesus gave Peter, John, and James special nicknames (Mark 3:13–17).

Paul referred to both Timothy and Titus as his sons (2 Tim. 1:2; Titus 1:4). He told the Thessalonians: "For who is our hope or joy or crown of exultation? Is it not even you, in the presence of our Lord Jesus at His coming? For you are our glory and joy" (1 Thess. 2:19–20). Paul's "crown," his greatest achievement, was seeing his beloved disciples following Christ faithfully. That is why he spent so much time investing in them. Let this be your goal as well.

Here are a few guidelines you may use as you invest:

> **Use various formats for discipleship.** There is no one magic formula to make a disciple. I have always used a combination of methods. You can have one-on-one meetings, phone calls, small-group meetings, video calls, and even larger retreats. In one of the retreats I hosted, sixteen guys came from nine states and one foreign country. For three days we studied the Bible, prayed for each other, shared meals, swam, and hiked a mountain. The guys loved connecting not only with me but also with each other. Through tacos, laughter, brotherly hugs, barbecue, and open sharing, lifelong friendships were formed. And we shed some tears when we said goodbye.

> **Be warm and relational.** Paul told the Philippians: "For God is my witness how I long for you all with the affection of Christ Jesus" (Phil. 1:8). When you gather your disciples, make it fun and inviting. You don't have to be overly serious or religious. Open your home and your heart and pour out joy. In an authentic atmosphere, your disciples will open their hearts, confess their struggles, and experience healthy growth.

> The apostle Paul stayed busy preaching, but people were his priority. He told the Corinthians he hoped to spend the whole winter with them! He said: "For I do not wish to see you now just in passing; for I hope to remain with you for some time, if the Lord permits" (1 Cor. 16:7).

> Paul made time for relationships. He planned his hectic life around his disciples. People were not "problems";

they were his priority. Paul had "so fond an affection" for the Thessalonians (1 Thess. 2:8), and he told the Roman believers: "Often I have planned to come to you" (Rom. 1:13). What would have happened if Paul had been too busy to visit or write letters to his disciples? Open your heart. Be intentional. Let God set your schedule. Let Him stretch you so you can contain a God-sized love.

Care deeply for those you are mentoring. Paul gave his disciples 100 percent of his life. He told the Ephesians that he invested in them "night and day for a period of three years" (Acts 20:31). He told the Thessalonians that he cared for them "as a nursing mother cares for her own children" (1 Thess. 2:7). He poured himself out whole-heartedly. He gave and gave and gave—at great personal cost.

What was the secret of this commitment? Paul said he invested sacrificially in the Thessalonians because they "had become very dear" to him and his disciples (1 Thess. 2:8). He cared so much he shed tears for them. You need the same depth of love for those you mentor. Don't be half-hearted or distant. Don't be a casual or part-time mentor. Give your all. Show real concern. Go the second mile. Love with all your might. Lay your life down for those you are called to encourage and inspire.

Expect to see results. Many years ago I started investing in a guy named Mike Foreman from Florida. We prayed together about his struggles in college. He was up and down when it came to some of his struggles, but I always tried to encourage him. I counseled him about his girl-friend. I listened and offered coaching when he left his job and became a pastor. I prayed for him a lot.

Mike eventually got married, had a family, and became the associate pastor of his church. One weekend when he came for a visit, we went to breakfast. I remember feeling proud of the maturity I could see in his life. I was able to tell him with all sincerity, "Mike, if I lived in your city I'd be happy if you were my pastor."

This is how discipleship works. As your disciple matures, your relationship will change. I still offer counsel, and I'll always pray for Mike as long as I live. But he grew up! He's a gifted leader who is making disciples of his own. The apostle Paul felt this joy of seeing men like Timothy and Titus become responsible leaders. Keep investing. One day you will feel overwhelming joy when your disciples surpass you!

The Third *I*—Include

Jesus' disciples listened to their Master's teaching constantly, but they were not sitting in a classroom. He taught on hillsides, in boats, in Peter's house, beside water wells, and during long journeys. But mostly the disciples learned by doing.

They watched Jesus interact with people. They listened to the compassionate tone of His voice. They saw Him touch lepers and apply clay to the eyes of a blind man. They were baffled when Jesus turned around in a crowd and asked, "Who touched My garments?" (Mark 5:30). They marveled when He overturned the tables of the moneychangers in the temple.

One day, during one of their many journeys along the shore of the Sea of Galilee, Jesus saw the growing crowd and asked His disciples how they planned to feed so many people. They were shocked by His question. "You want *us* to feed them? It would take the equivalent of eight months' wages to buy food for so many people."[1] (See John 6:7, NIV.) Jesus was planning to do a miracle, but He wanted to involve His disciples in the plan. He told them to search for food, and they came back with one meager meal—five loaves of bread and two pieces of fish.

After Jesus blessed the tiny lunch and began breaking it into pieces, He "kept giving them to the disciples to set before them" (Mark 6:41). Notice that Jesus did not just wave His hands over the food and magically create a smorgasbord for everyone. No, He instead kept giving the pieces of food to His disciples, and they carried the multiplied bread and fish to the groups of people who were seated on the grass. Jesus included His disciples in the miracle. They had a front-row seat that day, and they played a role in serving the most famous "fish taco" dinner in history!

As a disciple maker, this is your challenge as well. Your disciples will learn so much more by watching you than by just listening to you. They need to see how you spend time with God, how you study the Bible, how you share Christ with an unbeliever, how you pray for a sick person in the hospital, and how you counsel a depressed person at the altar of a church. Don't just teach a Bible study. Include your disciples in ministry opportunities. It is not enough for them to hear what you say; they need to see what you do.

Matthew 9 describes a very busy time in Jesus' life. In just a few days or hours, Jesus (1) healed a bleeding woman (vv. 20–22); (2) raised a girl from the dead (vv. 23–25); (3) healed two blind men (vv. 27–30); and (4) cast a demon out of a mute man (vv. 32–33). That's a lot of ministry! Then when Jesus saw more needy people coming to Him, He told His disciples: "The harvest is plentiful, but the workers are few. Therefore beseech the Lord of the harvest to send out workers into His harvest" (Matt. 9:37–38). Jesus was inviting His disciples to share the load. He was saying: "It's time for you guys to do what I do."

Some immature leaders want to be the star of the show. They want everyone to come to them for prayer. They want to wave their hands over the cheering crowds to boost their egos, while everyone else sits and stares. But that is not the Jesus way. When Jesus saw the crowds getting bigger, He brought His disciples onstage. He empowered them to join in His work. Don't do ministry to draw attention to you. Crucify your ego. Share the workload, empower others, build a team, and watch God multiply you.

When God first began opening doors for me to travel and preach, my wife could not go with me because some of our daughters were still living at home. I didn't want to travel alone, so I invited a few of the young men I was discipling to accompany me. This became a pattern. Within a few years I had taken dozens of young people on overseas mission trips as well as to domestic ministry engagements.

As much as I loved preaching in a church or conference, I realized that I enjoyed the time with my disciples even more than the public ministry. It was a powerful training experience for them, and we always had special times of fellowship and prayer during the events. Not only did they see God moving powerfully, but they also stayed with me and ate all their meals with me, so they were able to ask questions and receive personal mentoring for days. Now I cannot imagine going on a ministry trip without a "sidekick" to enjoy the journey with me. I believe this is the New Testament model of discipleship.

Years ago I developed a relationship with Roque Santiago, a Puerto Rican pastor who lives in Harrisburg, Pennsylvania. Everyone in his church has a Puerto Rican heritage, and they taught me to love *tostones, mofongo, pasteles,* and other Puerto Rican dishes. After Roque traveled with me once to preach in Guatemala, he fell in love with that nation. So when it was time for me to return to Guatemala to host a men's conference, I invited some of the men from his church, First Bilingual Christian Church of Harrisburg, to accompany me. I also asked them to teach in some of the conference sessions.

This was a huge challenge for these Hispanic men. Some of them had never been out of the country before. Some had never preached to a large audience. And they were certainly not used to the challenges of life in a developing country.

But Roque, Gerardo, and Hector stepped out of their comfort zones and ministered to the Guatemalan men in a small town near Zacapa. They prayed for countless guys at the altar, they shared their testimonies of spiritual freedom, and they witnessed grown men weeping and repenting for abusing their wives or neglecting their children. All the men from First Bilingual

Christian Church came home from that trip transformed because they had been included.

Many leaders today are actually afraid to include their younger disciples in ministry moments because they don't want anyone else to be in the spotlight. We are so insecure that we fear people might like our disciples' preaching more than ours! This is tragic. As long as we hold on to power and never give our disciples opportunities to grow, they will never venture out to do great things for God.

Several years ago I prayed for a young guy named Sam Kyle at his church in Pittsburgh. He was a high school senior, but I continued investing in him during his college years. He went with me on ministry trips to Puerto Rico and Tennessee, and we stayed connected. After he graduated he became a leader in an international missions program. Eventually I invited him to speak at one of my men's conferences when he was only twenty-four. To this day he is the youngest guy to ever speak at one of my events, and I am so glad I could give him that chance.

You must learn to open doors for your disciples. Don't block them. Encourage them and release them! Don't devalue them because they are inexperienced. Believe in them. Give them chances to succeed and they will spread their wings and fly. Paul told Timothy: "Let no one despise your youth, but be an example to the believers" (1 Tim. 4:12, NKJV). Paul saw Timothy's potential, and instead of being jealous he pushed him to greatness. You can do the same for young champions who want opportunities to grow.

In 2017 I took my friend Hao Xu on a trip to Guatemala. Hao is a native of China, but he found Jesus while he was a university student in the United States. I met him while he was studying at a ministry school in Pennsylvania, and he asked me for mentoring.

During our trip to Central America, I didn't want Hao to just watch while I preached. I told the church that Hao loves to pray for the sick and that he has seen many miraculous healings. The people were fascinated because Hao was the first Chinese man to ever visit that small community. They lined up for prayer at the end of each service, and some people experienced healings. Hao's faith was boosted, and he grew several feet spiritually because he had been given an opportunity to make a bigger spiritual impact.

On one of my trips to the nation of Iceland I invited two guys to join me, Mike Coretti from Canada and Alex Latis from Romania. I asked both men to speak at a retreat, and they did an exceptional job. Alex seemed surprised when I asked him to preach because he was not used to that kind of opportunity at home. But I enjoy pushing my disciples into deep waters so they can learn to swim. After Alex spoke I told him he was a gifted, compassionate leader, and he replied, "No one has ever told me this."

This kind of affirmation should be the norm. Our disciples need to hear us cheering them on. Jesus not only gave His disciples opportunities; He told them they would do more than He did. He said: "Truly, truly, I say to you, he who believes in Me, the works that I do, he will do also; and greater works than these he will do; because I go to the Father" (John 14:12).

If you are a secure leader, you won't be jealous if your disciples surpass you. If they preach better than you do or get more results, that's great! Wash their feet, encourage them, let them stand on your shoulders, and be proud of them when they receive applause. Let your ceiling become their floor, and push them higher. This is Jesus' way of mentoring.

The Fourth *I*—Instruct

God's Word is the heart of discipleship. If we want to follow God faithfully, we must learn His Word. We must be faithful students. We should cherish the Word, submit to it, honor it, and fearfully respect the author of it. We should treat it like no other book on earth, because it is "living and active" (Heb. 4:12). It is inspired by the Holy Spirit, and it has the power to change us when we read it.

Dawson Trotman, the legendary founder of The Navigators organization and a true expert on discipleship, said this about the importance of the Bible in the lives of the early followers of Christ: "I suppose there was no greater secret than that these men were in the Book and the Book was in them. The Word of God is the mighty force within that enables men to do whatever it says. I am absolutely convinced that the Bible completely changes the lives of men and women....It has completely changed my life. I'll never be the same again since I was introduced to God's Holy Word, the Bible."[2]

No man or woman can be a faithful disciple of Jesus if they are not lifelong students of the Bible. We must be in the Book, and the Book must be in us. There is no other way to become a strong Christian. And I have never known a strong Christian who didn't regularly wear out their Bible. If you want to be an effective disciple maker, encourage your disciples to become so voraciously hungry for Scripture that they can't live without it.

When I was eighteen I visited a woman named June Leverette at her home in Atlanta. She was a member of my church, and she invited me to have a conversation about how to go deeper in my relationship with God. When she opened her Bible I was shocked because I had never seen so many markings and hand-written notes.

June had underlined verses on every page, some in black and some with yellow, blue, or pink highlighters. She had obviously pored over every page, and the Teacher—the Holy Spirit—had revealed special truths to her as she studied. Just looking at June's colorful, dog-eared Bible that day inspired me to become a faithful student of God's Word. Today, decades later, many of the pages of my Bible resemble hers.

June did not just enjoy her Bible; she treasured it. It was like an antique box full of priceless, jewel-studded heirlooms. Through her reading and study she mined nuggets of gold and silver and precious stones, and those costly revelations became hers. June imparted that love of Scripture to me—and today I inspire my disciples to embark on their own excavating adventures, digging into the Word for life-changing insights. My life has become an adventure of discovery. I want to see Jesus come alive in every page of the Bible.

If you have this same voracious appetite for Scripture, your disciples will too. But you must cultivate that hunger first. The apostle Peter said:

> Like newborn babies, long for the pure milk of the word,
> so that by it you may grow in respect to salvation, if you
> have tasted the kindness of the Lord.
>
> —1 PETER 2:2

Peter could not have coached his followers to fall in love with Scripture unless he was in love with it himself. But he knew the Word. He had pored over the scrolls; He also heard the Master quoting it constantly. The Word was in him, and he passed it down to his spiritual son, Mark (1 Pet. 5:13). And Mark gave us the Gospel of Mark, which is based on Peter's personal testimony of Jesus.

When I begin discipling new believers, I always encourage them to study the Gospel of Mark first because it is refreshingly simple. It is the shortest Gospel and the most fast-paced account of Jesus' life. The word *immediately* appears in it about fifty times because Mark emphasizes the actions of Jesus more than His teachings. I have read it countless times, perhaps more than any other book of the Bible, because it vividly portrays the life of the Savior with powerful simplicity. Because I tasted of this "milk" of the Word, I have been able to share it with many others.

Your job as a disciple maker is to inspire those you are mentoring to become students of the Scriptures. How can you do that?

Make sure they have a good study Bible. When I studied the plays of William Shakespeare in college, I didn't read just the original texts from the late sixteenth century. If I had had to rely only on the original wording, penned in archaic Elizabethan English, I would not have understood half of it. Take this quote from *Romeo and Juliet,* for example: "Good night, good night! Parting is such sweet sorrow, that I shall say good night till it be morrow."[3] If I didn't have notations at the bottom of the page telling me that "morrow" was an old-fashioned way of saying "tomorrow," I might be confused.[4] And what about this line from *King Lear*: "Thou whoreson zed, thou unnecessary letter!"[5] What does that mean? Without study notes I would never know that "whoreson zed" refers to the fact that the letter *z* was rarely used in the sixteenth century. In the scene of the play, the Earl of Kent is telling his servant that he is unneeded.[6]

The Bible was written by forty different writers over a period of fifteen hundred years. Some of the ancient Hebrew in the Books of Genesis and Job is difficult to translate into modern English. This is why the notations and study aids in our Bibles are so crucial for readers today. Make sure your disciple has what he or she needs to become a good student.

Teach your disciple to use Bible study tools. When I was in college I learned how to use a concordance, which lists every word in the Old and New Testaments and gives the original Hebrew and Greek meanings. This information allows any reader to dig deeper for the nuance of meanings of a verse. In the 1970s, *Strong's Exhaustive Concordance of the Bible* was a 1,770-page tome that would seriously hurt you if it fell on your head. Today you don't have to lug that massive book around—it is easily accessible online. The same is true for *Matthew Henry's Commentary on the Whole Bible* and any good Bible atlas. You must teach your disciples how to use these tools in their study.

Do a Bible study with your disciple. Near the end of Paul's life, in what many believe was his last epistle, Paul tells Timothy: "When you come bring the cloak which I left at Troas with Carpus, and the books, especially the parchments" (2 Tim. 4:13). Scholars believe the "parchments" mentioned here were parts of the Old Testament. Paul was obviously engaged in a research project— some scholars believe he was writing the Book of Hebrews at this time, but we don't know for sure.

I would love to have watched the scene after Timothy arrived with this treasure of books and scrolls. Paul was obviously immersed in his study, and when these books arrived (hopefully before the cold, damp winter began) he likely shared with Timothy what he was learning. Can you imagine listening to Paul as he shared his revelations? Paul gave his disciple a deep love for the Scriptures. You can do the same.

The Fifth *I*—Intercede

The apostle Paul's communication with his disciples was limited. There were no smartphones, phone signals, shortwave radios, or even telegraph machines. Instead the apostle had to write letters that were carried on horseback, by hand, or by ship or chariot. His messages must have taken months to arrive at their destinations. Yet he told the Colossians: "I am with you in spirit" (Col. 2:5). He carried his disciples in his heart always. He told Philemon: "I thank my God always, making mention of you in my prayers" (Philem. 1:4).

It must have been extremely difficult for Paul to be separated from the disciples he loved. He would go to a new city, make a group of new converts, and spend months or years with them. He knew them by name and cared for them deeply. Then he would have to leave, either because of an outbreak of persecution or because the Holy Spirit directed him to evangelize a new region. I imagine he experienced many tearful goodbyes. But wherever he went he carried his converts in his heart. He prayed for them continually. He told the Ephesians:

> For this reason I too, having heard of the faith in the Lord Jesus which exists among you and your love for all the saints, do not cease giving thanks for you, while making mention of you in my prayers; that the God of our Lord Jesus Christ, the Father of glory, may give you a spirit of wisdom and of revelation in the knowledge

of Him. I pray that the eyes of your heart may be
enlightened, so that you will know what is the hope of
His calling, what are the riches of the glory of His inheritance in the saints, and what is the surpassing greatness
of His power toward us who believe. These are in accor-
dance with the working of the strength of His might.

—Ephesians 1:15–19

Prayers for his disciples seemed to pour effortlessly out of
Paul. He reflects the heart of a protective father who longed for
his children to know and experience all that God had purchased
for them. And Paul's prayers were not casual or haphazard; he
was focused and intense. He compared his intercession for the
Galatians to birth pangs. He wrote: "My children, with whom I
am again in labor until Christ is formed in you" (Gal. 4:19).

It might be safe to say that the early church was shaped in the
"womb" of the apostle Paul, who groaned in the anguish of tra-
vailing prayer until the first-century Christians reached a level
of maturity and strength. He wrestled in deep intercession, ago-
nizing because they faced the dangers of heresy, temptation, and
martyrdom.

Don't ever romanticize the New Testament church—our spiritual forefathers suffered horribly during those dark days, and
ministry was like warfare for them. Life is so much easier today,
but we are still involved in a serious struggle. I believe God calls
all of us to intercede for our disciples with the same determina-
tion and commitment that Paul modeled.

I've learned that disciples are formed in the forge of Spirit-
anointed prayer. Even though I invest in my disciples in many
ways, including one-on-one meetings, group sessions, retreats,
calls, and texts, prayer is the most important investment I make
in them. I keep a "visual prayer list" in my phone, with photos
of my family, mentors, friends, and disciples. I use it daily when
I pray.

Seeing their faces keeps them constantly in my thoughts. I've seen miracle answers to prayer—healings, engagements, babies born, churches planted, and countless spiritual breakthroughs. Don't just talk to your disciples about God. Talk to God about them!

Every day, in my prayer time, I look in my phone and see the faces of people I love. I pray for my wife, my four daughters, my sons-in-law, and my grandchildren. I pray for my mentors and my close friends.

I scroll through photos of my Timothys, and I pray for Abdiel, Igor, Diego, Alvin, Raja, Hani, Prasanna, Kevin, Paul, Dante, Kelechi, Godfrey, Lyle, Atu, Carlos, and Esdras. I pray for Doug, Jovanny, Cameron, Brian, Paul, Ben, Lyle, Jabin, Juan, Brian, Shannon, Omar, Joseph, Joel, Yoni, Antione, Doyle, Sam, Susheel, Mich, Helgi, Alex, Minase, Mehari, and Merhawi. I call out the names of Alvin, Dakotah, Anibal, AJ, Brandon, Jason, Luke, Leon, Tyler, Jesse, Julian, Mich, Kaylah, Tony, Charity, Fanny, Elijah, Badin, Israel, Mario, Alver, Shannon, Justin, Jason, Samson, Evan, Enrique, Nadim, Nori, Otoniel, Luis, Rolando, Adolfo, Adam, Arthur, and Vitaliy. I don't want to forget anyone!

Paul told his spiritual son Timothy: "I constantly remember you in my prayers night and day" (2 Tim. 1:3). Like Paul, I want to remember my disciples in prayer. That's why I use photos to help me pray. Seeing the faces of people in my smartphone reminds me of how much I love them.

Sometimes I spend more than an hour a day just praying for their needs. But I am also aware that prayer helps form a person into Christ's image. I ask the Holy Spirit to work in their lives, answer specific requests, and strengthen them with God's grace and power.

The prophet Samuel said: "Far be it from me that I should sin against the Lord by ceasing to pray for you" (1 Sam. 12:23). If God has put disciples in your life, you have a parental responsibility to pray for them. Let God use you to nurture and shape them into powerful followers of Jesus.

The Sixth *I*—Impart

When Paul spent time with his disciples, something spiritual took place called "impartation." He wrote to them: "For I long to see you so that I may *impart* some spiritual gift to you, that you may be established" (Rom. 1:11, emphasis added). The Greek word for *impart* means to "share" or "give."[7] In English, impart can mean to give a share of your possessions.[8]

When you are with a disciple you transmit truth and spiritual grace to him or her. You do this not only through preaching but also by telling your life experiences, admitting your weaknesses, letting them see your ups and downs, sharing what God has taught you from the Bible and from life, and praying together. But impartation is a bit different from investment. Impartation involves the supernatural work of the Holy Spirit. Notice these important words written to Timothy by Paul:

> This command I entrust to you, Timothy, my son, in accordance with the prophecies previously made concerning you, that by them you fight the good fight.
>
> —1 TIMOTHY 1:18

> For this reason I remind you to kindle afresh the gift of God which is in you through the laying on of my hands.
>
> —2 TIMOTHY 1:6

In both these cases we see that something of a spiritual nature happened to Timothy. He received prophetic words of encouragement as well as the infilling of the Holy Spirit. We aren't told whether Paul is the one who prophesied to Timothy—but it sounds as if Paul was there when these powerful utterances were made.

In the second passage we know it was Paul who laid hands on Timothy to receive the baptism of the Holy Spirit. Obviously these encounters were mountaintop moments for the young

Timothy, who needed God's promises and His power to fulfill his ministry in a very challenging situation.

I can't imagine the fear Timothy must have felt when he agreed to pastor the first New Testament church in the city of Ephesus. It was a demonic nest of idolatry and immorality. The spiritual warfare must have been intense. Many of the Jews there were hostile to the gospel, and according to Acts 19:28–29, the pagans were even more resistant. Paul knew that Timothy could not reach that dark stronghold with only intellectual knowledge of the Scriptures. Timothy needed spiritual weapons. He would need to fast, pray, and preach with the anointing of the Spirit. He was hopeless without heaven's power.

There will be times when you will need to pray for this kind of impartation of divine power for your disciples. Don't shy away from this. I cannot count how many times I have laid hands on my Timothys and asked God to fill them with courage, faith, and miraculous anointing. I have asked Jesus to wrap His mantle around them and give them a double portion, just as Elisha received from Elijah. (See 2 Kings 2:9–13.) I have declared words of prophecy over them that they could keep in their arsenals— strong words that became like implements of battle.

I will never forget the day I prayed for my friend Matt Hyde, a young pastor in Boise, Idaho, whom I have mentored for several years. After spending a day together talking about the challenges he faced at his church, Matt and I stood together in his den at his house, and I laid hands on his back. I could see in the invisible realm that the Lord was straightening his back and inserting what looked like a metal rod in his spine.

I knew the Lord was imparting confidence and strength to face future battles. God was calling Matt to be strong and courageous, just as He commanded Joshua before he invaded Canaan. (See Joshua 1:9.) I cannot explain how impartation works, but I know that God released a spiritual power that day into my friend Matt's life. After we finished praying we both knew God had done something significant.

As you spend time with your disciples, there will be moments of divine impartation. Be ready to be a vessel of the Holy Spirit. Make sure your lamp is trimmed and your oil bottle is full. Be prepared to prophesy. He wants those you mentor to be armed with spiritual gifts and weapons so that they become victorious warriors.

LET'S **PRAY** ABOUT IT

Lord, help me to identify the specific people You want me to disciple. Then give me Your grace so I am able to invest in them, include them in practical training experiences, instruct them in Your Word, intercede for them regularly, and impart the life of Your Spirit to them. Make me a channel of Your power so they can become strong men and women of faith. Amen.

ONE **FINAL** THOUGHT

Ministry sounds intimidating until you develop a realistic view of what ministry is really about. Maybe you're not gifted to preach sermons, start a rehabilitation clinic, or lead a marriage retreat. But do you know people who struggle with sin? Do you know people who are carrying burdens? If so, then your first steps toward ministry are easy: help them.[9]

–FRANCIS CHAN, AUTHOR, *FORGOTTEN GOD*

DISCIPLESHIP TIP
Learn to Invest Time in People

I love to read about the apostle Paul's journeys—not just because of the adventure, the miracles, and the narrow escapes, but also because of the way Paul modeled relational discipleship. He invested so much time in those he mentored. The Bible says Paul and his team "spent a long time with the disciples" in Antioch (Acts 14:28). When they visited the church in Troas, Paul and his team "stayed seven days" (Acts 20:6). When he landed in Tyre, he looked for the disciples and stayed with them for another seven days (Acts 21:4).

Discipleship is a time investment. You have to make it a priority. Don't shortchange those you mentor. And remember that you can give your time even if you are not present with them. You can call, text, or email. Paul was not always with his disciples, but he wrote to them—even from prison!—and his letters make up a lot of the New Testament. His investment in them lives on today.

CHAPTER 8

A Disciple Maker Is a Servant

I N 2012 I spoke at a conference for young men in Kampala, Uganda, with my friend Medad Birungi, a leader in the Anglican Church who had introduced the power and gifts of the Holy Spirit to very traditional churches. The three-day event was held at an Anglican retreat center, so we had access to a cafeteria for meals, dormitory-style rooms, and a nice auditorium for our teaching sessions. When I arrived I also noticed that the facility had a swimming pool, which was not common in Kampala.

During the first session Medad explained to the men that we would have discipleship sessions in the mornings and evenings and time for recreation in the afternoons. Since the weather was hot and I wanted to get to know the students, I suggested that we all go swimming in the pool. Several of the guys agreed to meet me there at 2:00 p.m. But when I arrived I noticed that all the young men were standing along the edge of the pool, and no one was in the water. They all seemed hesitant—maybe even a bit frightened.

"Why is nobody in the water?" I asked.

"We've never been in a swimming pool," one of the guys replied.

"There are no swimming pools in our village," another one said.

"We do have rivers and lakes where we live," said another. "But there are crocodiles in the water." His comment solicited some nervous laughter.

After I assured everyone there were no dangerous reptiles in the pool, I asked my new friends how many of them knew how to swim. No one raised his hand. So I immediately offered to give swimming lessons.

I had learned to swim at age nine in a lake at a Boy Scout camp in Alabama, so I knew how to float, kick, and do the breaststroke—and how to teach other people as well. The guys sheepishly ventured into the water, giggling like little kids as they splashed each other. By the third day I had taught several of these guys how to dogpaddle or float on their backs. And in the process I won their trust—because nobody spotted a single crocodile in that water!

At the final lunch of the retreat, I sat down at a table with some of these young men and asked them to share their highlights of the three days. They had listened to numerous sermons, and we had enjoyed special times of worship and prayer in the evenings. I wanted to know what they had learned. But the feedback at that table surprised me.

"What really blessed me the most was that you were with us," one brother said.

"*With* you?" I asked. I wanted more explanation.

"In the past, when American preachers came here, they just preached and then went into a private room," another said. "They did not spend time with us. I loved that you sat with us, and you wanted to know us."

I was choking back tears at this point.

"And I loved that you taught us how to swim," said another. I remembered that this brother had struggled a bit when I told him to relax, as he was trying to float and kick his legs at the same time.

Those comments marked me forever because I saw in those Ugandans a longing for true relational discipleship. I'm sure they loved my sermons during that week, but it wasn't the sermons that impressed them. I'm sure they loved the powerful moments of prayer we had at the altar in the evening, but that is not what stood out. In the end, what these young men needed was a relationship with a father figure.

Don't Call Me "Bishop"

Several years after the Uganda trip, while I was preaching in the nation of Iceland, I befriended three young foreign students from Africa who were visiting our conference near Reykjavik. I noticed these guys were sitting in the back of the auditorium, so I invited them to sit with me up front. They later admitted to me that I was the first preacher they'd ever met who greeted people individually before a service.

"In my country, most preachers come into the auditorium after the worship, and they don't speak to anyone. They just appear from behind the stage," one of the brothers told me. When I told these guys they could call me Lee, they were shocked. They expected me to demand a fancy ecclesiastical title.

I'm often asked if I have a title, and my answer doesn't satisfy some people. I don't consider myself a pastor because I travel so much. All kinds of labels have been pinned on me: reverend, prophet, apostle, minister, and even bishop.

Once I was introduced to a church as Dr. Grady, and I almost crawled under my seat. I have only a Bachelor of Arts degree from a liberal arts college in Georgia. I don't have an MDiv, a DMin, or a PhD degree. There are no letters after my name. God didn't lead me to get any advanced theological degrees.

Today it seems we've developed a title fetish. For a while everyone in charismatic church circles was becoming a bishop, and some were installed into this office with rings, robes, and funny-looking hats. Then the same guys with the pointy hats started calling themselves apostles. Then the prophets got jealous and started calling themselves apostles too. I knew one famous woman preacher who, not to be outdone, required people to call her Exalted Prophetess.

A few years later the fad changed, and church folks began to require titles—as in, "When apostle Holy Moly arrives, please only address him as Apostle, and then make sure he is seated in a private room while his two 'armor-bearers' guard his door." I know of one popular preacher who sends his hosts a letter explaining that he must be addressed as Apostle anytime his name is used from the stage. (He also requires certain standards of luxury in his hotel, including special mineral water.)

Some of these title seekers have invented an elaborate theology to go along with their ridiculous rules and requirements. They say you can't receive the true anointing from a man of God if you don't honor him with his right title. To some people this sounds so very *oooh-oooh* spiritual. But it's garbage.

Jesus didn't play this religious game, especially when He was around the Grand Poobahs of His day—the long-robed, nose-in-the-air scribes and Pharisees. After accusing them of loving the best seats in the synagogues, He pointed out that they loved to be called Rabbi by men. (See Matthew 23:6–7.) Then He warned them: "But do not be called 'Rabbi,' for you have one Teacher, the Christ, and you are all brothers....For he who exalts himself will be humbled, and he who humbles himself will be exalted" (Matt. 23:8–12, MEV).

People have quibbled over these words for centuries, insisting that pride is what Jesus was rebuking, not titles. I would agree that Jesus was going to the root sin. But He was also asking these guys if they'd be willing to ditch their fancy labels and act like normal people. He was asking them to come down to earth, where real ministry happens.

When I was in China several years ago, I met some amazing leaders who had planted thousands of congregations. They had also spent a lot of time in jail for their faith, and they'd been beaten with iron rods for preaching the gospel. Some had even been subjected to electric shock treatments. They were the bravest apostles I've ever met.

But when I asked them if they used "apostle" as a title, one guy said: "We believe in those roles in the church. But we prefer to call each other 'brother' or 'sister.'"

That settled the issue for me.

If these Chinese giants of the faith—and true apostles—don't require to be addressed with titles, then Your Worshipful Grand Master Rev. Dr. Bishop Big Deal Jones who claims oversight of four churches shouldn't wear his ministry role around his neck like a tacky neon name badge.

I'm not saying people shouldn't use reverend, minister, or even bishop to identify their roles in the church. One of my mentors, Doug Beacham, is a bishop in his denomination—and he is one of the most humble men I know. But can we please dispense with the insecurity and the childish "I'm more important than you" appellations and get back to the simplicity of the gospel? Let's get over ourselves!

Jesus is the King of kings, the Lord of lords, the Son of David, the Prince of Peace, and the Apostle of our confession. Yet when He came into this world, He laid aside His heavenly glory and took on the lowly name of Jesus. He wore no fancy robes. He demanded no titles. He had no armor-bearers. He even bore His own cross until He was too weak to drag it to Calvary.

If you want to serve Jesus honorably, you must forsake your need for fame and cast your crowns at His feet. And if you want to be an effective disciple maker, you must become a servant. You must recognize that the highest level of spiritual ministry may not be preaching or prophesying or healing the sick; it may be washing another person's feet, serving someone a meal, or visiting a sick person in a hospital.

Or, in my case, teaching some young Ugandan men how to swim.

The apostle Paul was one of the greatest leaders in history. But he didn't act like a celebrity or demand to be served. He wasn't focused on building his own ministry. He said, "I will most gladly spend and be *expended* for your souls" (2 Cor. 12:15, emphasis added).

The Greek word for *expended* means "to spend oneself out for others."[1] This is what you must do as a leader. It's not about you. Lay your life down for your disciples. Invest until you are totally poured out. Then let God fill you up so you can pour yourself out again.

The older I grow in the Lord, the more precious the bond I feel with those I'm mentoring. This is the wondrous love of God. Even though I am not their natural father, I sense a deep affection and parental connection with them.

Paul referred to Timothy as his "true child in the faith" (1 Tim. 1:2) and his "beloved son" (2 Tim. 1:2). He also called the slave Onesimus "my child" (Philem. 1:10), and he addressed Titus as "my true child in a common faith" (Titus 1:4). Paul had deep love for his disciples because he had adopted them into his heart.

Love makes discipleship easy because it flows out of God's supernatural love, not out of religious duty. Ask God for a true father's heart and "adopt" your disciples without reservation. Your love will be a tangible expression of the Father's love.

Keep Your Feet on the Ground

John the Baptist said he was not worthy to untie Jesus' lowly sandals (Mark 1:7). But in today's hyper-cool, megachurch culture, a preacher's footwear has become very pricey. So pricey, in fact, that an Instagram account called PreachersNSneakers went viral in 2019 and as of this writing has 269,000 followers. The social media account offers photos of famous preachers' expensive and colorful footwear—including a pair of red Air Yeezy 2s worn by South Carolina pastor John Gray. One pair of his designer shoes retailed for $5,611.[2]

Some people have complained about the Instagram site, claiming that its founder—a guy named Benjamin Kirby—is hurting the church's reputation. But he says he's simply holding up a mirror and asking Christians if our leaders should be known for their lavish tastes in clothes.

There's really nothing new about this. In the 1980s,

televangelists were criticized for their three-piece suits and pricey Italian leather dress shoes—and we know their followers gave them enough money to buy private jets. Today the suits and leather shoes are out of date, but the price tag on the designer sneakers is the same.

In today's vocabulary it's called swag. It basically means stylish confidence, and it comes from the word *swagger*. Like the televangelist of the old days, the celebrity preacher of today may still be on television—or he may have his own YouTube channel. But his look has been totally updated. His hairstyle is hip, he has a few days' stubble on his face, and his ministry has an app for your smartphone. And apparently his onstage wardrobe must now include a pair of $1,000 Air Jordans.

I'm not against hair gel, stubble, or the latest designer athletic shoes. I enjoy some of these preachers' podcasts. And in their defense, some of these men received their fancy footwear as gifts from wealthy donors. But I am concerned about the swag factor. Technology and youthful trendiness can breed pride if we're not careful. And pride is still pride, whether it is clothed in yesterday's neon polyester or today's ripped jeans.

As ministry platforms grow larger, the potential for bigger egos grows more dangerous. If we want to make disciples as Jesus did, all of us need to take a humility test. If we are going to create a culture of relational discipleship in the church today, we need less swag and more brokenness in the pulpit. You can't invest in people sacrificially if you spend all your time calling attention to yourself. You can't disciple someone if you are looking down on them from your lofty seat.

Let's remember these basic biblical principles as we choose whom to follow:

Christians should never worship preachers. Paul rebuked the people of Lystra when they called him and his companion, Barnabas, gods. Paul told the people, "We are also men of the same nature as you" (Acts 14:15). True ministers of God will not allow their followers to place them on pedestals. Paul knew that his proper role as a bondservant of Christ Jesus was to take the lowest seat. (See Philippians 1:1.) He also knew that ministers must never allow flattery or adoration to inflate their egos.

Preachers must know who they are and who they aren't. When some of John the Baptist's disciples pointed out to him that Jesus was also baptizing and that everyone was going to Him (see John 3:25–26)—as if Jesus had usurped John's place— John assured them: "You yourselves bear witness of me that I said, 'I am not the Christ,' but 'I have been sent before Him....He must increase, but I must decrease'" (vv. 28–30, MEV). Even some of the most gifted Christian communicators can be seduced by the power of technology—and the roar of a crowd—so that they actually believe they are in an elite category. No! We are nothing, and He is everything. We must get out of the way so people can see Jesus.

Leaders who have not crucified the lust for self-promotion can become infatuated with the big and the sensational. They can build big churches with bigger projection screens, yet their character cannot sustain the pressure of spiritual warfare that inevitably comes. An out-of-control ego becomes a monster. Author Henry Blackaby said it this way: "Nothing is more pathetic than having a small character in a big assignment. Many of us don't want to give attention to our character; we just want the big assignment from God."[3]

Ministry is best accomplished through a team, not a celebrity. Paul laid the foundations of the church in the Gentile world, but he always shared the spotlight with Timothy, Silas, Barnabas, Titus, Phoebe, Priscilla, and other coworkers who suffered in prison with him and faithfully preached alongside him. He didn't try to be five places at once; he trained people to take his place. And nobody on the team had swag.

It is becoming popular for large churches to open satellite campuses that offer video sermons from the same preacher. If this strategy is effectively reaching more converts, that's great. If preachers can do that and stay humble, keep it up. But let's be careful that we are not building ministry on one man's charisma. Our ultimate goal should be for a whole new generation of people to be trained and empowered to serve, not for one man to build a show around his gift—and certainly not around his expensive Air Jordans.

Don't Ever Become an Exploiter

If you are going to be a healthy mentor, you must allow God to burn out of you all wrong attitudes of leadership. You must become a true servant. Only those who have a heart of humility can lead others in a Christlike way.

My friend (I will call him Greg) wanted a mentor. He was eager to learn the ropes of ministry, so he asked an older pastor in Ohio for training. The pastor agreed—but Greg soon realized the man wanted a valet, not an apprentice. Greg became the man's armor-bearer, a strange term used in some churches to describe a ministry intern.

The man never took Greg on hospital visits, didn't involve him in ministry assignments, and never prayed with him. Instead Greg was expected to carry the pastor's briefcase, fetch his coffee each morning, and take his suits to the cleaners—with no salary offered. In this case *armor-bearer* was a spiritualized term for *slave*. This is *not* biblical mentoring!

This bizarre armor-bearer trend became popular in churches more than twenty years ago, but unfortunately it's still practiced in some circles. It appeals to insecure leaders who need an entourage to make them feel important. This type of leader is infected with a virus that I call *egotisticus giganticus.* Pride has caused his head to swell. He is incapable of discipling someone because he is too worried about impressing people—and retaining his position. He lacks the capacity to serve. He is not a discipler; he is an exploiter.

I have never had an armor-bearer, and I don't need one. When I turned fifty, I decided to spend most of my energy investing in the next generation. This became my passionate priority because

I met so many gifted men and women in their twenties and thirties who craved mentors. Many of them, like Greg, were looking for authentic role models but could find only self-absorbed narcissists who were building their own kingdoms.

If you want to be a healthy mentor, please make sure you are not infected with the armor-bearer virus. Take these steps to adjust your attitude:

1. **Get over yourself.** Today's insecure leaders don't realize it's the devil tempting them to become rock star preachers. Fame is too alluring. Before they realize it their heads have swelled to the size of Godzilla, and ministry has become a means to prove their imagined greatness. A leader with an inflated ego will have zero interest in investing in others. You must tell yourself daily: "It's not about me!"

2. **Stay accessible.** Young people today don't want just our sermons. They want to sit down for coffee after the sermon. They want to ask questions. They can listen to a hundred preachers on YouTube, but when you invite them to dinner, offer to pray with them, or take them on a mission trip, you mark them forever.

3. **Keep it real.** Older Christian leaders have picked up bad habits that turn off young people. Some ministers preach with affected voices, demand celebrity treatment, or manipulate audiences in weird ways to pretend they have a powerful anointing. Please talk in a normal voice when you preach so young people won't dismiss you as a fake. Be transparent, admit your faults, and let everyone know you've had struggles. Young people don't want to follow someone who pretends to be perfect.

4. **Pour on the encouragement.** Many young people today struggle to stay disciplined. Some have

addictions. And many of them have immature attitudes. But you will never reach them if all you do is point out their faults. You have to win their hearts before you address problems. If you saturate them with the love of a caring father or mother, their spiritual growth will amaze you.

5. **Don't cling to power.** Elijah gave a double portion of his mantle to Elisha (2 Kings 2:9–13). Jesus was the Son of God, yet He willingly handed His authority over to His disciples and told them to finish the job (Matt. 28:18–30). Paul handed his baton to Timothy when he finished his race (2 Tim. 4:1–8). This is the biblical model for leadership—a humble willingness to be surpassed by the next generation.

Every good leader should already be thinking of his or her succession plan. If you have a tendency to control, dominate, or manipulate people, you must wrestle with God until your ego is crushed. Let the Holy Spirit break you. Young people today don't want to follow people who strut and swagger. They are looking for mentors who walk with the limp of humility. Don't let the armor-bearer mentality fill you with pride.

A Key to Biblical Humility

Humility is a requirement for all who make disciples. But how do we acquire it? It is not the norm in the church today because we are so programmed to love the big performance. I believe the most vital thing we can do is prioritize "the one" over the crowd.

Once when Paul visited the Christians in the city of Troas, he preached so late—until midnight—that a young man named Eutychus dozed off, fell out of a third-story window, and died. (See Acts 20:7–9.) Some people can't handle long sermons—not even Paul's! The Bible says Paul "went down and fell upon him… embracing him," and Eutychus was raised to life (v. 10).

The Greek word Luke uses here is the same word used to describe how the father "fell on" the prodigal son in Luke 15:20.[4] This reveals the heart of true discipleship. Preaching to crowds is great, but Paul was willing to focus on one bored teen. I'm sure the crowd loved Paul's marathon sermon, but Eutychus received a life-changing hug and personal prayer. He was marked forever.

Who knows what became of that boy? He could have become a great apostle who took the gospel to Italy or Libya. Don't be so focused on the need for a crowd that you can't pay attention to the Eutychuses who are sitting in the back near the windowsill.

Imagine if this same Troas event had happened in twenty-first-century America. How would we write about it? To begin with, most people wouldn't even pay attention to a small meeting held in an upper room of a house. We would not be impressed with the size of that gathering. And we might not want to tell that a teenager fell out of a window since that might open the landlord to personal liability!

But the Bible places big value on small meetings and on sleepy teenagers who have powerful encounters with God. Don't be so focused on big numbers that you fail to value the one.

In 2014 I was invited to speak at a church in St. Louis. I didn't know the pastor at all, but I was happy to minister to his congregation. I don't remember anything particularly special that happened in the service, and I have never been back to that church. But after the meeting some of us went out for a late meal, and I met a young man named Brandon McPherson.

Brandon was serving as an associate pastor at the church, and he wasn't even in my meeting that night because he had to serve in the children's service. Over dinner at an IHOP, God connected me with Brandon. He was deeply discouraged at that time, and he was ready to throw in the towel. He felt defeated. But the Lord knit our hearts, and we have stayed close for years.

If I were focused on crowds, I would not have cared about meeting Brandon. After all, he didn't even hear my sermon! But God cares about the one. The Lord sent me all the way to

St. Louis to encourage a young minister who was on the verge of giving up. Today Brandon has planted a growing church in Virginia.

The apostle Paul preached to crowds, of course. But he spent most of his time with his disciples, and he gave special attention to Timothy. The result was that Timothy carried Paul's heart. Paul said of him: "I have sent to you Timothy...and he will remind you of my ways" (1 Cor. 4:17). Crowd ministry is necessary and can result in changed lives. But you will make the most lasting impact if you reproduce yourself in the one. Then, when you die, the next generation will carry on.

This is the Jesus way. If you learn to invest in the one, you will develop the humility needed to create a culture of discipleship everywhere you go.

LET'S **PRAY** ABOUT IT

Lord, I need the heart of a servant so I can lay my life down for the people You have called me to disciple. Break any prideful spirit in me. Forgive me if I have ever done ministry to be seen, to impress others, or to receive applause. Give me the heart of Jesus for people. Make me approachable and compassionate. And help me to care more about serving one person than about serving the big crowd. Amen.

ONE **FINAL** THOUGHT

At every step of our Christian development and in every sphere of our Christian discipleship, pride is the greatest enemy and humility our greatest friend.[5]

—JOHN STOTT, ANGLICAN THEOLOGIAN

DISCIPLESHIP TIP
How David Multiplied Himself

We all know David killed the giant Goliath. But we forget that near the end of David's life four more giants attacked Israel. David was old by that time, and he "became weary" in the battle (2 Sam. 21:15). Yet four of his loyal warriors stepped in, and they bravely killed the four giants (vv. 17–22).

These four mighty men—Abishai, Sibbecai, Elhanan, and Jonathan—each did what David had done years earlier. They were copying what they had seen their mentor do. David's courage inspired them. And he had trained them well. This story proves the power of biblical mentoring. When you make disciples your impact will be multiplied—and many more giants will be defeated!

My mentor, Barry, taught me years ago that Jesus had a four-step process for discipleship:

> ➤ "I do it." Jesus taught and worked miracles.

> ➤ "I do it, and they are with Me." Jesus ministered while His disciples watched and learned.

> ➤ "They do it, and I am with them." Jesus pushed His disciples to preach, heal, and cast out demons while He coached them.

> ➤ "They do it, and I encourage them from the background." Jesus handed over His work to us. Now we minister as His Spirit empowers us. Your job as a mentor is to work yourself out of a job!

CHAPTER 9

Practical Tips for Effective Mentoring

THE BOOK OF Mark is my favorite Gospel. I describe it as the best Gospel to share with teenagers—or with anyone who has a short attention span. It is the shortest account of Jesus' ministry and the most fast-paced. It is focused on Jesus' actions, not His sermons. If a movie were based on the Gospel of Mark it would be a noisy action film, complete with screaming demons, instantaneous healings, and rioting crowds.

But what I love most about the Book of Mark is the backstory of its author—who is sometimes referred to as John Mark. He is young when we first meet him in Scripture. He was related to Barnabas and closely associated with Peter. (Scholars believe Mark's Gospel is based on what Peter dictated to him.)[1] Yet Mark created an embarrassing dilemma for the apostle Paul. We are told that Paul separated from Barnabas in Antioch because Mark deserted the missionary team. (See Acts 15:37–40.)

We can only speculate about what caused this awkward conflict. We don't know why Mark went AWOL. Did he fear persecution? Did he wimp out because he missed his mother's cooking back in Jerusalem? Or did he go through a period of rebellion? Perhaps. But in the end the prodigal son came home. The epistle of Philemon says Mark began traveling with Paul again. (See Philemon 1:23–24.)

Paul eventually told Timothy: "Pick up Mark and bring him with you, *for he is useful to me for service*" (2 Tim. 4:11, emphasis added). *Useful* is putting it mildly. This young guy, who experienced failure early in life, later wrote a key portion of the Bible!

The lesson is clear: don't give up on young people. They are totally worth the investment, even if they encounter ups and downs and zigzags on the journey we call discipleship. Those of us who are in the "older" category must recognize how useful young Marks are in the plan of God. We can't give up on them. I can't help but wonder if Paul felt sorry for writing off Mark too soon.

I am blessed to have many young Marks in my life these days. The personal time I spend with them is just as important as any sermon I preach to a crowd. I have come to realize that when I invest in a young Christian, they carry what I give them into the future. Their impact will last long after I am gone.

The church is graying, and many young people have checked out because our approach to ministry has become irrelevant to them. We are too detached. We are too smug. We are stuck in outdated mindsets. Maybe, like Paul, we are too focused on the work at hand to give untrained trainees time to grow. We expect them to mature overnight. We aren't willing to be patient.

But if we will listen to their hearts, treat them like sons and daughters, invest our time in them, and recognize their gifts, they will—like John Mark in the first century—make an amazing impact on history.

The point of Mark's story is that discipleship is a challenging and messy process. It is ultimately rewarding, but it's also full of disappointments and headaches. You will often be tempted to quit—or to walk away from a disciple when God is calling you to stay committed to them.

I have experienced a wide range of problems in my years of mentoring, and people who are ready to throw up their hands and quit have asked me many questions. Here are just a few of the questions I've been asked, along with answers I've found in God's Word:

Q. How long should I disciple someone?

A. I never view discipleship as a short-term assignment. I want to stay connected to those I mentor for a lifetime. I've learned that relationships stay vibrant as long as I nourish them with regular communication.

As your disciple matures you will relate to each other differently. But never assume that your job is done; don't "drop" people out of your life. Even after Paul had fully trained Timothy and was aware he (Paul) would die soon, he urged Timothy: "Make every effort to come to me soon" (2 Tim. 4:9). Keep the bonds strong and develop lifelong relationships.

Q. Is it possible to disciple someone who is complacent or uninterested?

A. The Bible says that when Jesus said to Peter and Andrew, "Follow Me, and I will make you become fishers of men," they "immediately left their nets and followed Him" (Mark 1:17–18, NKJV). They were eager. They wanted what Jesus had, and they were willing to sell everything to get it.

Even though Peter had his weak moments, he passionately pursued Jesus and became a disciple maker. The same can be said for Elisha. When he chose to follow Elijah, he left his family farm and sacrificed his oxen as a sign of total commitment. (See 1 Kings 19:19–21.) And he eagerly pursued his mentor up until the moment Elijah was carried into heaven in a flaming chariot (2 Kings 2:1–11).

If someone is reluctant, distracted, or lacking spiritual motivation, you're wasting your time. Invest wisely. You must look for hungry people who are willing to make sacrifices to be a disciple. Yes, keep sowing your seed freely among the crowds, but spend most of your time training the sincere Peters who will follow Jesus no matter what. They will become world changers.

This doesn't mean you give up on a disciple if they miss one meeting or forget to read the assigned chapter in a book study. Some people have to develop discipline. But pay attention to the heart motivation. If the person you are trying to train is half-hearted, your seed will likely fall on hard ground. It would be better to invest in someone who is motivated.

Q. How many people can I mentor?

A. There is no magic number. Your capacity to make disciples is largely determined by the time you have available. If you have a strenuous job or a young family, you will not have as much time as a person who is single or semiretired. Don't feel bad if you have only one or two disciples.

This is not a contest. You can disciple only as many people as God gives you the grace for. Let Him show you the size of your "quiver" for spiritual sons and daughters.

I also believe you can mentor people at various levels. Jesus called twelve men to follow Him closely, and He discipled a group of women (Luke 8:1–3). He also trained a group of seventy in ministry (Luke 10:1), and He preached to crowds (Matt. 5:1). But Jesus invested more time in three of His twelve disciples (Peter, James, and John), and John seemed to have the deepest revelation of the Savior because he had such close access to Him.

Jesus did not invest the same amount of time in everyone. He influenced people on different levels, but He focused on the few. Don't spread yourself too thin. No matter how many people you influence, make sure you invest your quality time in the small number of disciples God has put closest to you.

Q. Can a man mentor a woman, or a woman mentor a man?

A. In the Bible we see men mentoring men (Paul and Timothy), women mentoring women (Naomi and Ruth), men mentoring women (Jesus and Mary Magdalene), and women mentoring men (Priscilla, along with her husband, Aquila, taught Apollos, as recorded in Acts 18:26). Titus 2:3–4 encourages older women to disciple younger women, especially in how to manage their families.

A mature Christian can be a spiritual father or mother to younger believers of either gender, but there are times when men need input from men and women need input from women.

If I am training women disciples, I prefer to meet with small groups of them rather than with a woman alone. This is out of respect for my wife and to avoid "all appearances of evil" (1 Thess. 5:22, MEV). I'm also careful about where we meet. Jesus met with the Samaritan woman in a public place—not a private office. Use wisdom. And if you ever feel you are battling temptations in a mentoring situation, talk about your struggle with a mentor or friend. Stay on your guard, know your heart, and never allow a discipleship relationship to become romantic or sexual.

Q. Is it OK if I show my own weaknesses to my disciple? How vulnerable should I be?

A. Paul had a close relationship with his disciples. He mentored them, but they also refreshed him and ministered to him. A mentoring relationship is not a one-way street. As a mentor, never pretend that you are Superman or Captain Marvel. Be real.

Paul was a model Christian, but he admitted that he had a "thorn in the flesh" (2 Cor. 12:7). He boasted about his weaknesses because this helped him lean on the power of Christ (v. 9). Don't be a fake. Be an authentic, approachable mentor who bleeds, cries, limps, and fights with temptation. Your authenticity will give others hope.

Several years ago when I preached in South Africa I felt the Lord tell me to share a very embarrassing experience from my past. I didn't want to tell the story because I was afraid people would think less of me. But I felt I should be brutally honest. As

FOLLOW ME

a result many men came to the altar and admitted to having a similar experience.

If you are transparent in the pulpit, people will be more likely to confess their sins. You must lead the way. No one wants to hear a pompous preacher who brags about his money, his cars, or his accomplishments. If you act perfect people won't relate to you. The apostle Paul said: "I will rather boast about my weaknesses" (2 Cor. 12:9). A humble preacher will produce humility in those who listen to him.

Q. Is there a financial cost to discipleship?

A. My father taught me the principle of generosity. He always tithed to his church, but he was also generous with me. He paid for my first car and for my college tuition. After he became an old man he always insisted on paying for the meal if we went to a restaurant—even when I had my wife and our four children with us.

When I began mentoring my disciples, I often took them to coffee shops or restaurants. I always insisted on paying the tab—even when some of the guys would fight me for the check. And I quickly learned that God always rewards us for generosity, even when it's something as simple as paying for a cappuccino or a Waffle House breakfast.

A few years ago when I was preaching in Florida, I invited eight guys I've mentored to a special dinner. I encouraged them and listened to their prayer requests, and then we prayed for each other. Afterward I paid the one-hundred-dollar bill for our meal.

The next week a friend handed me a check for one hundred dollars. I thanked him, and then I asked the Lord what it was for. I sensed the Holy Spirit say, "That's your discipleship money." I didn't even know there was such a thing as "discipleship money," but it encouraged me that the Lord was keeping track of these expenses. He is involved in the details of our lives!

Paul told the Corinthians: "I will most gladly spend and be expended for your souls" (2 Cor. 12:15). Discipleship will require lots of time, energy, love, and money—but you cannot put a price tag on the reward of seeing your disciples growing spiritually. I have no idea how many thousands of dollars I have spent on meals for my disciples—or how much in other funds I have wired to my Timothys overseas. But I know that God blesses discipleship.

Q. How do you structure your time with those you are mentoring?

A. There is no one right answer to this. You can be flexible and creative, but my time has been invested in five basic formats: 1) face-to-face meetings—these are best for me, but sometimes I do a "video coffee break" with someone by way of a call on FaceTime, WhatsApp, or Skype (I also do lots of phone calls and texting); 2) small groups, usually between two and twelve people; 3) ministry trips, during which my disciple has full access to me on the journey; 4) group retreats, during which a small number of disciples gather for a weekend of ministry and close fellowship; and 5) normal life activities. The most powerful moments of impartation happen spontaneously—especially over a meal, during a mountain hike, at a swimming pool, or at the gym. Down time with your disciples is a priceless gift.

Q. How do you keep your disciples motivated?

A. Healthy discipleship is soaked in sincere love. It is not cold or professional. You invest in people not out of duty but because God has knit your heart to them. Paul expressed this love in words. He didn't just feel it—he said it!

I try to tell my disciples three things constantly: "I love you," "I'm proud of you," and "I'm so glad we are connected." As a mentor you must let God's love flow out of you like a gushing river!

For years I have sent my disciples a weekly text about discipleship to encourage them. I send them individually (not as a group text) because discipleship is a very personal process. Disciples are handmade, not manufactured on a factory assembly line. I take the time to send these messages one by one because I care about them.

Q. How should I confront my disciple if he continually falls into sin?

A. Your disciples need constant encouragement. But there are times when you must say some hard things. You may have to correct or even rebuke. Paul said we must "speak the truth in love" (Eph. 4:15, NLT). If all you do is soothe, comfort, and affirm your disciples, you aren't loving them. Love also confronts.

I want to be a loving mentor, but I can't be soft on sin. Confrontation is like surgery: it must be done with precision and care. Don't be a butcher who slashes with a sharp knife. When you cut, do it in a way that brings healing. Your disciple will thank you for it later, even if it hurts.

But you must also learn to minister correction with heavy doses of grace. The word *grace* appears in the New Testament approximately 122 times (in the New American Standard Bible; 156 times in the King James Version).[2] Paul says "Grace to you" at the beginning and closing of most of his epistles. And the last verse of the Bible says, "The grace of the Lord Jesus be with all. Amen" (Rev. 22:21). Grace does not imply leniency toward sin. But it reveals that God is always willing to forgive and restore because He is a compassionate Father.

Always trust in God's grace as you mentor others. It's not up to you to change people. You are not the Holy Spirit. You can instruct, encourage, and correct, but God's life-giving power is working in your disciples. Expect to see powerful changes. As the Spirit works they will defeat sinful habits, grow in faith, develop character, and discover their spiritual gifts. You will see miracles!

You can't show grace to those you are mentoring if you haven't accepted grace yourself. As a mentor your life should also be soaked in grace. Start your day thanking God for His love and forgiveness. End your day praising Him for His blessings. We don't deserve to be saved. Yet God loved us anyway and extended grace to us. Forgive yourself. Meditate on the fact that the Father loves you in spite of your mistakes, habitual sins, and weaknesses. When you know His amazing grace in a deeply personal way you can extend it to others.

Q. What keeps you motivated to keep investing in your disciples?

A. Sometimes we can grow tired of mentoring people. It's hard work! It involves many meetings, phone calls, listening to problems, and offering counsel. It can be draining when your disciples ignore your advice or make bad choices. How do you stay motivated to keep investing in them?

Paul had a secret. He loved his disciples as if they were his own children. He told the Thessalonians: "Having so fond an affection for you, we were well pleased to impart to you not only the gospel of God but also our own lives, because you had become very dear to us" (1 Thess. 2:8).

When you have this kind of warm, God-sized love for those you are discipling, you'll never give up on them. You'll keep pouring into them and patiently praying for them until they are spiritually mature. Love is the secret.

Q. How can I minister to my disciple when he or she is going through tough times?

A. Your disciples will face tests, trials, and temptations. They will have what I call "freak-out moments." They may even pull away from you because they are discouraged. Here are a few of the steps I take in these situations:

- **Give them space.** You aren't God, and you can't fix their problems. Don't hover or smother. Step back, knowing that the Holy Spirit will step in.

- **Stay calm.** Don't overreact, scold, or get upset because of their problems. Gently remind them you are available to chat.

- **Pray for them.** Jesus knew His disciples would scatter after He went to the cross. He prayed: "Holy Father, keep them in Your name" (John 17:11). Pray protective prayers. Engage the enemy, and fight for them!

- **Share a word of hope.** Isaiah 50:4 says: "The Lord GOD has given me the tongue of disciples, that I may know how to sustain the weary one with a word." One word from God can break heaviness. Let God use you to bring hope and comfort.

Q. What do you do if one of your disciples pulls away from you?

A. Your disciple may be going through a wilderness of discouragement like David; he may feel guilty because he gave in to temptation like Peter; he might even be running from God like Jonah. Do you just wait until he contacts you? Or do you chase him down?

The most important thing you can do is pray. Ask the Holy Spirit to work in his situation. Then let him know you are praying and that you are available to talk. He may not respond immediately, but he needs reassurance of your love. Even if he doesn't answer the phone you can text or leave a message.

Demonstrate that you love him unconditionally by not scolding him, getting offended, or cutting him off. Remember: "Love is patient" (1 Cor. 13:4). Keep loving; keep pursuing; keep encouraging even when your disciple is going through hard times.

Q. If you are discipling someone, do they also need to be in a local church? Or does your discipleship meeting take the place of church?

A. I never, ever consider my meeting with a disciple as a replacement for the local church. I am providing vital input into the life of the people I mentor, but they also need to be connected to the family of God.

Many Christians have a "me and Jesus" attitude. They think Christianity is simply a vertical relationship. They pray, read the Bible, and listen to popular podcasts or worship music, yet they aren't involved in a local church. Or if they are, they don't build close friendships. But Christianity is not just vertical—it's horizontal.

Hebrews 10:25 warns us about being mavericks. It says we should not forsake "our own assembling together, as is the habit of some." The primary reason we gather at church is to strengthen one another.

Paul told his friend Philemon: "Yes, brother, let me benefit from you in the Lord; refresh my heart in Christ" (Philem. 1:20). God wants to use you to benefit and refresh others! Don't close your heart to God's family. Don't be an isolated Lone Ranger. Form tight bonds of fellowship with your brothers and sisters in Christ, and help your disciples find the support of a loving church community.

Q. How do I help my disciple if he or she keeps falling into the same sin?

A. I hear this question often, especially about the issue of pornography because it is such a pervasive problem. If your disciple is struggling with porn or other sexual sins, of course you can enlist an accountability partner, get a filter on his computer, or suggest a course in purity. But those things won't help until your disciple makes a powerful choice. He must decide to resist.

Titus 2:11–12 says God's grace has come, "instructing us to

deny ungodliness and worldly desires." *Deny* in this verse means "not to accept, to reject, to refuse something offered."[3] It is a powerful *no*. And it takes a real backbone to say no. If you are constantly giving in to temptation, your backbone is weak and your spiritual muscles are flabby. You must begin intense resistance training.

I always counsel my disciples that they must never allow porn or other temptations to turn them into mushy, jellyfish Christians. I challenge them to grow a spine. They must put their foot down. They must veto the devil and refuse the cravings of the flesh.

I learned a long time ago in the gym that resistance training is the only way to build muscle. Whether you do push-ups or lift weights, you must resist if you want to stimulate muscle growth. The resistance breaks down muscle fibers, and when they grow back they increase the size of the muscle.

The same is true spiritually. You must resist the pressure of temptation if you want to build spiritual muscle. James 4:7 says, "Resist the devil and he will flee from you." Resisting makes you strong in the Spirit. But muscle gain takes time.

If your disciples are tempted in any area, they have two choices. If they resist, they will grow stronger and develop character and purity. If they give in to temptation, they will stay flabby and weak. I always remind those I mentor that if they learn to resist the devil, they will become ripped, shredded warriors!

Sometimes shame will prevent your disciple from confessing their problems. Recently one of my young disciples asked if we could talk. He wanted to confess something from his past, but he was afraid to open his heart. I waited patiently until he was ready to be vulnerable. When he told me about his sin (which happened several years prior) he was shaking, but he finally confessed it.

As a mentor you must be prepared for such moments. Don't act shocked when your disciple confesses something. Don't scold, scowl, gasp, or judge. Show genuine concern and then pray. Galatians 6:1 says: "If anyone is caught in any trespass, you who are spiritual, restore such a one in a spirit of gentleness."

God's heart is restoration, not condemnation. I always remind my disciples that they are cleansed by Jesus' blood. I look them in the eyes and tell them there is no record of their sins. Their debts are paid in full. When they know true forgiveness they will grow spiritually.

Q. What if my disciple decides to walk away from God?

A. Even the apostle Paul discipled people who chose to leave the faith. One of those was Demas. Paul called Demas a "fellow worker" (Philem. 1:24), but later Demas abandoned Paul. The apostle tells us: "Demas, because he loved this world, has deserted me" (2 Tim. 4:10, NIV). We don't know why Demas abandoned his faith (perhaps he was afraid of persecution?), but this situation reminds us that discipleship can be painful.

If you invest in a person and then they reject Christ, you may be tempted to blame yourself. Or you may feel like pulling back from mentoring others because you don't want to be hurt again. But Paul did not let Demas' failure stop his mission. Neither can you. It's OK to shed tears over those who backslide because you care for them deeply. But don't let your disciple's wrong choices derail you. Take the risk. Keep pouring your life into others.

Also, make sure the person who walked away knows that you are available in case they ever decide to return to the Lord. Even though you may no longer be meeting with them regularly, it's OK to check up on them from time to time. And you can continue to pray for them. Prayer is an eternal investment, and the answer to yours could come after you have stepped into eternity.

Q. Sometimes I feel exhausted after spending time with my disciples. Is this normal?

A. I always feel poured out after I preach or minister for a few hours. Spiritual ministry will take a lot out of you. This is also true when you counsel your disciples, pray for them, or lead a Bible study. When you pour yourself out spiritually you will feel depleted. Ministry is spiritual labor, and the exhaustion you experience might even make you feel depressed. Don't be surprised by this. It happened to Paul, David, and Elijah. It's a normal response when human vessels carry God's power.

When you preach, lead worship, organize an outreach, disciple others, or go on a mission trip, the Holy Spirit's anointing pours out of you. Afterward you need to be replenished. After Elijah called down fire from heaven he became depressed and hid in a cave. He slept, ate, and slept some more before his next task. (See 1 Kings 19:4–8.)

After ministering you need physical, mental, and spiritual rest. This does not mean just reading the Bible and praying; you need sleep, food, family time, recreation, and hobbies. Always take the necessary time to relax and let God refill you.

Never gripe about your disciples pulling on you. Be grateful that God has considered you faithful enough to put these special people in your life. When you are poured out, the Holy Spirit will replenish your strength. And remember that God does not forget your sacrifice. Hebrews 6:10 says: "For God is not unjust so as to forget your work and the love which you have shown toward His name." Keep investing. Keep encouraging. You will see a reward.

Q. What are the biggest mistakes you've made in mentoring?

A. I've made plenty of mistakes over the years while investing in my disciples. I have also seen other mentors make big mistakes, so I've kept a running list of things to avoid when I'm helping others grow spiritually. Thankfully I have avoided many of the blunders on this list. Here are the top ten biggest mistakes I hope you will also avoid:

1. **Ignoring communication from your disciples.**
   Discipleship requires your time. Answer calls or
   texts and make sure your disciples know you are

accessible. You don't have to drop everything to take a call, but let them know when you can call back.

2. **Acting disgusted if your disciples confess serious sin.** True emotional healing requires transparency and repentance. But you must show mercy and sensitivity when your disciples decide to bare their souls. Never, ever condemn them.

3. **Breaking your disciples' confidence.** I've met Christians who closed their hearts and even stopped going to church because a pastor or mentor blabbed about confessions they shared privately. If the person you are mentoring trusts you enough to admit their deepest struggles, be a faithful steward with that information. It is not yours to share with anyone else.

4. **Babying your disciples.** You must treat your disciples as adults. Don't coddle them or spoil them. The apostle Paul said: "When I became a man, I put away childish things" (1 Cor. 13:11, NKJV). You'll never lead people to spiritual health if you treat them like kids. Expect growth and maturity.

5. **Avoiding confrontation.** In this era of "hyper-grace" theology, some Christians have backed away from any form of tough love because they're afraid of appearing narrow-minded or legalistic. You must get over this fear. If you truly love your disciples, you will lovingly but firmly correct them when necessary.

6. **Controlling or manipulating.** You are not running your disciples' lives. Your job is to help them hear from God for themselves—not to hear from God for them.

7. **Being possessive.** Your goal as a mentor is to serve your disciples and help them grow. But you are not

the only person they need in their lives. Leave room for friends and other mentors, and don't be jealous if they go to someone else for help.

8. **Allowing the relationship to become codependent.** You must always point your disciples to Jesus. Don't allow them to develop an unhealthy reliance on you. And never try to get your own emotional needs met in a discipleship relationship.

9. **Exploiting your disciples financially.** Over the years I've met pastors or mentors who asked their mentees to join their "downline" in a network marketing business or to invest in buying clubs or foreign currency schemes. This is a huge mistake. Using a mentoring relationship to enrich yourself contradicts everything Jesus said about purity of heart. It is inappropriate for you to ask your disciples for money.

10. **Giving up on your disciples.** Can you imagine Jesus kicking Peter to the curb after he denied Him? No, Jesus didn't disqualify Peter for his sin—He restored him. Stick with your disciples during good times and bad, even if they have serious moral failures. Love them, forgive them, and never stop praying for them. Be a mentor for a lifetime.

LET'S **PRAY** ABOUT IT

Lord, I choose to lean on You as I begin the adventure of discipling others. I know I don't have all the answers. I need wisdom! James 1:5 says that if any of us lacks wisdom, we can ask You, "who gives to all generously… and it will be given" to us. Thank You in advance for showing me how to face each challenge, and please give my disciples special grace whenever I make mistakes. Amen.

ONE **FINAL** THOUGHT

You are not here in the world for yourself. You have been sent here for others. The world is waiting for you![4]

—Catherine Booth, Cofounder, The Salvation Army

DISCIPLESHIP TIP
Keep Sowing and You Will Reap

Discipleship requires a lot of work: counseling sessions, one-on-one meetings, small-group meetings, phone calls, texts, and hours of prayer. And it's frustrating when a disciple stumbles into sin, loses his spiritual fire, or pulls away from you. Paul told Timothy: "For I am already being poured out as a drink offering" (2 Tim. 4:6). I can relate to his description. Sometimes I feel poured out!

But I refuse to complain about the workload of discipleship. Never gripe about your disciples pulling on you. Be grateful that God has considered you faithful enough to put these special people in your life. When you are poured out, the Holy Spirit will replenish your strength. And remember that God does not forget your sacrifice. Hebrews 6:10 says, "For God is not unjust so as to forget your work and the love which you have shown toward His name." Keep investing. Keep encouraging. You will see a reward.

Sometimes you may sow for a long time without seeing results. You may grow weary and question whether your labor is making a difference. You may be tempted to quit. Be assured that God sees. He turns tiny seeds into crops. Keep sowing in faith, even on days when the ground is hard. God always brings a breakthrough. Psalm 126:5 promises that "those who sow in tears shall reap with joyful shouting."

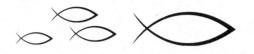

CHAPTER 10

Returning to the Book of Acts Model

IN EARLY 2021 I preached at Crossroads Church, a thriving mega-church in Newnan, Georgia, near Atlanta. Crossroads has a Southern Baptist affiliation, but the worship is more passionate than it is in many charismatic churches I've visited. The church packs huge crowds into its sanctuary on weekends, although when I was there most of the people were masked and socially distanced because of the coronavirus pandemic. But the COVID-19 outbreak didn't stop this church from reaching their community.

The most unique thing about Crossroads is its commitment to small-group ministry. During any given week people take part in more than two dozen healing ministries—offering everything from divorce recovery to grief counseling to freedom from addictions or sexual abuse. New believers gather in small groups so they can grow in their faith.

The church's pastor, Ken Adams, loves to preach the Word from his pulpit, but he's an unusual leader because he believes Christians can't grow without small groups and close relationships. He's not the star of the show, and that's OK with him. He knows Sunday morning church isn't enough. That's why he had organized a discipleship summit for the weekend I visited to encourage his members to embrace the call to biblical discipleship.

During the summit, my mentor of forty-seven years, Barry St. Clair, asked me to join him on the stage. We sat on stools and told the story of how he invited me to be a part of a small youth discipleship group when I was only fifteen. I shared with the audience how Barry not only taught me the basics of the Christian life but also modeled what it means to make disciples. His humble example inspired me to spend most of my adult life mentoring younger people. Now my disciples do the same.

When I was at Crossroads that weekend I could sense that what was happening there was not an isolated phenomenon; it was evidence of a sweeping tsunami that promises to reshape the church in the years to come. All across this nation and the world, the COVID-19 pandemic forced us to reevaluate our core priorities. We have been divinely disrupted.

I don't believe God sent a virus to kill people; sickness is from the devil. But God can use anything to change us. He works all things together for the good of those who love Him. (See Romans 8:28.) Just as the noisy winds of Pentecost brought sweeping changes two thousand years ago to the early church, heaven has shoved us into an uncomfortable realization that going back to business as usual will not work. (See Acts 2.)

Looking back, I can see that God used this painful international crisis to prune away dead branches so that we can bear more fruit. (See John 15:1–2.) The shift has begun whether or not we are ready for it. I've described some of the ways the Holy Spirit is renewing our wineskins so we can contain what He is sending. (See Mark 2:21–22.)

We are shifting from quantity to quality. In the days before COVID we assumed we were successful if we had big crowds in a nice building. But the apostle Paul said ministry made with wood, hay, and stubble will burn up when tested by God's holiness. (See 1 Corinthians 3:12–13.) Just because a sanctuary is full of people doesn't mean we are making strong followers of Jesus. We must never evaluate our success by worldly standards. God is not impressed with crowds; He wants strong, faithful followers who can influence others.

We are shifting from spectators to disciples. Churches that already had strong small-group ministry before the pandemic stayed strong during the crisis and rebounded afterward. But churches that put all their resources into big congregational events were shut down or lost huge percentages of their membership. Church-growth expert Thom Rainer predicted in 2020 that 20 percent or more of marginal churchgoers (who were not connected to any small group) would never return after the COVID-19 crisis.[1]

Jesus didn't call us to make churchgoers. He never intended for His followers to just sit in pews year after year, listening to the same sermons and being entertained. He told them, "Go therefore and make disciples of all the nations" (Matt. 28:19). He certainly did not want His followers to remain spiritual infants; He invites us all to grow up and do the works that He did.

We are shifting from big events to small groups. There's nothing wrong with big gatherings. I love to worship with a crowd. But when we made the church about the crowd, we created a monster that doesn't resemble the early church described in the Book of Acts. People don't grow effectively if their only input comes from a weekly or monthly thirty-minute sermon. They need solid discipleship training in a close-knit environment with supportive relationships.

We live in a world full of fear, loneliness, and abuse. And that's a big reason many people would never set foot in a big church full of strangers. Their social anxiety prevents them from walking into a concert-style arena to hear a sermon. But they would consider visiting your home for a meal or a small-group study. Why are we making it so hard for people to connect?

We are shifting from unapproachable celebrities to accessible servants. We have lived through the era of the rock star preacher, and this fad is fading fast. It is no coincidence that during the COVID-19 pandemic of 2020 and 2021, several high-profile ministers with massive followings literally disappeared because of tragic moral failures. I didn't rejoice when I heard the news about these leaders because I know we are all capable of making horrible mistakes. But the collapse of these giant ministries underscored the fact that God is calling us away from Hollywood-style glamour and back to New Testament humility.

True ministers of the gospel don't allow people to make them the focus. Jesus is the star. When we embrace the idea that all Christians can make disciples—not just the most eloquent or the highest paid—we will impact the multitudes as the early church did.

Ministers who lead as Jesus did aren't afraid to empower others, and they aren't afraid that their followers may become more successful than they are. In fact, they want their disciples to surpass them. The faster we shift away from the celebrity model, the sooner we will reach the world with Christ's love.

Jesus never commanded us to "go ye therefore and attract crowds." He called us to *"make disciples"* (Matt. 28:19, emphasis added), and that cannot be done exclusively in once-a-week meetings, no matter how many times the preacher gets the people to shout or wave handkerchiefs. If we don't take immature Christians through a discipleship process (which is best done in small groups or one-on-one gatherings), people will end up in a perpetual state of immaturity.

David Kinnaman, coauthor of the excellent book *unChristian*, articulated the problem this way: "Most people in America, when they are exposed to the Christian faith, are not being transformed. They take one step into the door, and the journey ends. They are not being allowed, encouraged, or equipped to love or to think like Christ. Yet in many ways a focus on spiritual formation fits what a new generation is really seeking. Transformation is a process, a journey, not a one-time decision."[2]

Reclaiming this process of discipleship is going to require a total overhaul of how we do church. Do we really want to produce mature disciples who have the character of Jesus and are able to do His works? Or are we content with shallow believers and shallow faith?

A friend of mine had to face this question while he was pastoring in Florida. As a young father, he had a habit of putting his infant son in a car seat and driving him around his neighborhood at night in order to lull him to sleep. Then, after the boy finally got quiet, the father would tiptoe into the house and lay the child in his crib. Once during this ritual the Holy Spirit spoke to the pastor rather bluntly while he was in the car. He said: "This is what you are doing in your church. You are just driving babies around."

My friend came under conviction. He realized he had fallen into the trap of entertaining his congregation with events and programs, even though the people were not growing spiritually. He had been content to keep them in infancy. As long as they filled their seats each Sunday and paid their tithes, he was happy. Yet no one was growing, and they certainly were not producing fruit by reaching others for Christ.

In the first century, the apostle Paul was frustrated with the immaturity of his followers in Corinth. He rebuked them in his first letter to them:

> And I, brethren, could not speak to you as to spiritual men, but as to men of flesh, as to infants in Christ. I gave you milk to drink, not solid food; for you were not yet able to receive it. Indeed, even now you are not yet able, for you are still fleshly.
> —1 CORINTHIANS 3:1–3

Paul didn't enjoy being a babysitter. He was called to mentor leaders who would grow up and learn to shake nations for Jesus Christ. I don't know if those Corinthian Christians ever grew up; the Bible doesn't tell us. But we face a similar challenge today.

Youth ministry expert Winkie Pratney wrote more than fifty years ago: "Too many church-goers are not channels, but sponges. Their entire philosophy is self-centered. Their world revolves around good to themselves, instead of good to others. They ask God for blessings, but fail to realize that a 'blessing' cannot truly bless until it has been passed on."[3]

When God called Abram to leave his family and his Mesopotamian idols to follow Him (Gen. 12:1), He said these words: "And I will make you a great nation, and I will bless you, and make your name great; and so you shall be a blessing" (v. 2). Then in the next verse He restates the promise by saying, "And in you all the families of the earth will be blessed" (v. 3).

Over the years I have heard many preachers talk about the blessings of Abraham. They have promised their congregations wealth, cars, mansions, private jets, summer homes, winter homes, flourishing businesses, and even winning lottery tickets. This is a childish, fleshly way to interpret the Abrahamic promise.

The ultimate point was not that Abraham would be rich; the point was that he would become a channel of blessing to others. God was saying, "I will bless you so you can bless others." This is the essence of maturity—to grow to such a place of generosity and servanthood that we are willing to invest all that we have to help others.

I'm sure there will always be prosperity preachers who dangle sugarcoated spirituality in front of juvenile crowds. But many Christians today are feeling sick from this junk food diet. They crave the deeper things of God. They want the meat, not the milk. They want to grow up and become givers, not takers. They don't want to *hoard* the blessing; they want to *give* the blessing.

How do we wean selfish Christians off this "give me" mentality? How do we encourage spiritual growth? How can we create a culture of discipleship in our churches?

- Churches must stop focusing exclusively on big events and get people involved in small groups, where personal ministry can take place.

- We must stop treating people like numbers and get back to valuing relationships.

- Leaders must reject the "celebrity preacher" model and start investing in the lives of individuals.

- All Christians must realize that it's not only the pastor's job to disciple—it is *every* believer's job!

When we stand before Christ and He evaluates our ministries, He will not be asking us how many people sat in our pews, watched our TV programs, followed our Instagram accounts, or filled out response cards. He is not going to evaluate us based on how many people recited the sinner's prayer or how many healings we counted in each service. He will ask: "How many faithful disciples did you make? How many people did you influence for Me? Did you move beyond *receiving* blessings and learn to *be* a blessing?" I pray we will make this our priority.

Small Groups Are God's Idea

I love large worship gatherings when God's people assemble to sing and celebrate. There's really nothing like worshipping with hundreds or even thousands of Christians. King David wrote of the exhilaration of corporate assembly. He said: "I will give You thanks in the great congregation; I will praise you among a mighty throng" (Ps. 35:18). In David's time such huge gatherings were probably held on Old Testament feast days, which occurred seven times a year.

We enjoy the thrill of large corporate meetings today, and they are enhanced by skillful musicians, modern sound equipment, and wide screens with graphics. Our worship has come to define the modern American church—and there's nothing wrong with that.

But if all we offer is big, concert-style events, we are missing an essential part of the New Testament church's life. During the time of the Book of Acts, early Christians didn't meet just for worship in the temple. They met in small groups to learn, fellowship, pray, and eat.

> So those who had received his word [Peter's sermon on the day of Pentecost] were baptized; and that day there were added about three thousand souls. They were continually devoting themselves to the apostles' teaching and to fellowship, to the breaking of bread and to prayer....Day by day continuing with one mind in the temple, and breaking bread *from house to house,* they were taking their meals together with gladness and sincerity of heart.
>
> —ACTS 2:41–46, EMPHASIS ADDED

Jesus had already ascended into heaven, so He didn't give specific orders to divide the crowd into smaller groups. His disciples somehow knew this would be a more effective strategy. Perhaps they remembered when Jesus fed the crowd of five thousand. On that day Jesus commanded His followers to "sit down by groups on the green grass" (Mark 6:39). So "they sat down in groups of hundreds and of fifties" (v. 40). Then He blessed the bread and fish and distributed it to everyone (v. 41).

The early apostles intuitively understood that if they were going to effectively disciple a group of three thousand new believers, they would not be able to do it in a crowd setting. The people needed personal attention and individualized instruction. They needed to be able to see the teacher up close, ask questions, and connect with others over meals. And so, on the day the church was born, small-group ministry was instituted. This was the work of the Holy Spirit. It should remain the pattern for us today.

Discipleship would have been impossible if all the post-Pentecost converts had been herded into the temple for a sermon series. (The lack of a sound system alone would have made this impossible.) But Peter and the other disciples had learned from the Master that they needed to invest in the few. So they sent the people into various homes. I'm sure the 120 disciples who were filled with the Holy Spirit in the Upper Room on Pentecost (Acts 1:13–15; 2:1–4) were prepared to lead the discussions.

Many church leaders today are resistant to the concept of small-group ministry. They are addicted to big. They want to measure the number of people in seats. They crave the noise and excitement of the crowd. And, if we are honest, we will all admit that small-group ministry is hard work because it requires many trained leaders and can be an administrative headache.

It's a lot easier for one good preacher to speak to one thousand people than it is to train one hundred people to speak to groups of ten each. But when we take the time to invest in small-group ministry, the result is exponential growth and measurable maturity. Leaders grow because they are pushed beyond their limits; the people in the small groups grow because they have intimate, in-person instruction; and the groups multiply as people share their experience with others.

Imagine that you have a one-year-old baby, and you plan to drop her off at your church's day care center. When you arrive you walk into a cavernous auditorium where more than eight hundred babies are on the floor—on blankets, in car seats or strollers, or in baby carriers. The day care volunteers are walking around, offering bottles and diaper changes. They are consoling crying babies and tending to others that are fussy. Would you leave your child in that place?

Of course not! You can't take care of eight hundred babies in an auditorium. They need individual attention. They need to be separated into groups, preferably by age. You probably wouldn't want more than six to ten of them in the same room, with a high ratio of teachers to babies so the little ones will receive the proper care.

If this is true, why would we think it wise to herd eight hundred or one thousand new believers into a large church auditorium and assume they will mature properly? They must be in smaller groups. If the church is going to create a healthy culture of discipleship, we must devise a wise strategy of small groups to facilitate growth.

I am often asked for tips on how to lead effective small groups.

One of the most common questions I hear is: "How many people should be in a small group?" I have led groups as small as three and as large as twenty-five. There is no magic number, but it has to be small enough for people to connect. I personally recommend no more than twenty, but the Holy Spirit will guide you as you lead.

Here are some of the guidelines I use for effective small-group ministry:

Have a clear focus. If you start a group, you want to define the focus. Is it discipleship for new Christians? A Bible study for men? A Bible study for women? Is it for college students? There are many options—you can study a book of the Bible, study a Christian book, watch a teaching series on video, offer recovery resources for alcoholics, provide support for single mothers, or give aid to people who are grieving. State and restate your purpose often.

Invite the right people. If it is a group for new Christians, invite only those. If it is a group for young adults, don't change the formula. And if you are making disciples, make sure they are all hungry Christians who want to grow.

Don't invite footdraggers, people with cold shoulders, or the smug and satisfied. You will only be frustrated if you have to drag people along. Remember Isaiah 55:1: "Ho! Every one who thirsts, come to the waters; and you who have no money come, buy and eat. Come, buy wine and milk without money and without cost." You need to invite the hungry. It is impossible to disciple someone who doesn't want discipleship.

Plan your schedule. It is best to have beginning and ending dates for your meetings. Don't say, "We are having this Bible study every Wednesday night until Jesus returns." Use a semester model so you can reevaluate the need and the strategy.

Sometimes the Spirit will tell you that a group is finished. Don't get locked into anything forever. If a group is based on a book, you will be done when the book ends. If it is based on a book of the Bible, such as Mark, your study will run for sixteen weeks. A study on the Book of Acts might take twenty-eight weeks since there are twenty-eight chapters.

Get everyone involved. When you lead a group you are a facilitator. That means you don't do all the talking; you try to get everyone involved. You can do something as simple as asking someone to read a verse or say a prayer. The key is to get everyone talking and especially pull the shyest people out of their shells.

Make a point to affirm those who are reserved. There are times when you may talk the most, but you need to see your role as that of a musical conductor, involving all the instruments. Don't think of your group as an audience of spectators. This is why you want to sit in a circle rather than in rows as in a classroom. Proverbs 20:5 says, "A plan in the heart of a man is like deep water, but a man of understanding draws it out." As the leader you must seek to draw responses out of people, remembering that Jesus often asked His disciples questions.

Read the room. As a leader you must be perceptive. Don't be so focused on your lesson that you miss what is happening in the meeting. Some people are hurting. Some are carrying burdens. Some are distracted by stress. Some are lonely and looking for connection. In Matthew 9:4 it says Jesus knew what the Pharisees were thinking. You must rely on the Holy Spirit to help you lead. Pray before the meeting that you will be sensitive in the Spirit.

Don't allow hijackers. Sometimes certain people will try to dominate a conversation or make the lesson about them. Beware of attention seekers. Say things like, "Let's hear from someone tonight who hasn't said anything," or, "That's good, John. But let's let someone else share this time." You may also need to go to the hijacker privately and ask them to back off.

Also, be aware if someone is pushing a pet doctrine, political viewpoint, or false theology. Do not allow them to pollute the well. You may even have to correct them publicly.

Have a prayer time. You always want to encourage people to look to Jesus for His answers and miracles. This is preparing a way for the Lord. You can do this in many different ways: 1) Ask people to get in clusters of three; 2) ask three or four people to pray; 3) offer to close the meeting with a general prayer; 4) ask people to share prayer requests and then have everyone pray for them; or 5) offer a "hot seat" method, in which each person with a prayer request sits in a chair in the middle so others can surround them, lay hands on them, and pray.

Be hospitable. It is part of our human nature to want to gather around food and have times of fellowship. Food warms the heart and connects us. Some of Jesus' most significant times with His disciples involved food, including sharing the Passover meal and His last breakfast on the beach. (See Luke 22:14–20 and John 21:12–13.) Offering food will also encourage people to stay and connect after the small-group lesson.

Stay connected. Your work is not done after your group time is over. Stay in communication. Use text, phone, or social media to interact. Do follow-up and check on the group members. Show genuine concern.

Jesus spent time with the Twelve, but He also had one-on-one time with His disciples. Develop the heart of a shepherd who is willing to "leave the ninety-nine" (Matt. 18:12) to find the one. This is going the extra mile because your flesh will tell you that you've done your part by hosting the group.

Aim to multiply. If the Holy Spirit is working in your group, people will feel His impact. They will be inspired by the teaching. They will experience healing. They will be encouraged. And they will bring others. Growth will end up doubling the size of your group, and you will need to divide to keep it intimate.

Be aware that the Lord will raise up others to colead with you. You may want to designate a person to be a coleader in case you are not there. This person can be a potential leader of a new group. Throughout the process, expect to see God's supernatural multiplication.

God Breaks So He Can Multiply

When Jesus fed the five thousand as described in Mark 6:35–41, He did four things: 1) He *took* the bread and the fish; 2) He *blessed* the food; 3) He *broke* the food; and 4) He *gave* the food to the multitude. This is how God works with us. He *takes* us, He *blesses* us, He *breaks* us, and then He *shares His life* through us.

We all want to see miracles. And we all love the fourth step, when abundant food manifests—with more than enough to satisfy the crowd. But if you truly want to be used by God, you cannot skip the third step. We love to be *blessed*, but few of us want to be *broken*. Yet this is the path of discipleship.

If you have not been broken, you cannot reach your full potential. Your influence will be determined by how much you allow the brokenness of God in your life. God uses trials and difficulties to form your character. You must embrace your trials and let God shape you. You must submit to His dealings. If you let Jesus break you in His loving hands, your life will touch a multitude.

The story of the feeding of the five thousand gives us insight into how Jesus wants to use each of us. The Christian life is not about getting more for ourselves but about giving ourselves to others. This is how success is measured in the kingdom—not by what you have but by what you give.

Discipleship is a simple concept—maybe too simple for some of us who have become addicted to the bells and whistles of celebrity-focused religion. But if you listen carefully amid the distraction of the noisy crowd, you will hear the Holy Spirit calling us back to the simplicity of New Testament basics.

The book you are holding in your hands is dangerous. The message I have shared with you requires you to change. The call to biblical discipleship will totally reorder your priorities, reconfigure your schedule, and force you to change old habits. Jesus told us that if we want to be fruitful, we must go through a pruning process. He warned us, "Every branch in Me that does not bear fruit, He takes away; and every branch that bears fruit, He prunes it that it may bear more fruit" (John 15:2).

Jesus was sharing an uncomfortable truth in this verse. If we want to grow spiritually, and if we want more spiritual fruit, we must submit to the Father's plan, not ours. He has to cut things away so new growth will appear. He might need to prune things we cling to. We can't just skate along in comfort, always getting what we want. If we desire the fruit of a mature Christian life, we must welcome change.

British preacher Charles Spurgeon, when preaching about John 15, said: "All the fruit-bearing saints must feel the knife."[4]

I don't like the knife! Pruning is an ugly, painful, and embarrassing experience. If you've ever seen a row of pruned trees, you know what I mean. Grapevines that have been pruned are cut back so drastically they look dead. When I cut back the rosebushes in front of my house, they look naked and exposed. Are you willing to live the pruned life? Consider these realities:

Pruning cuts off what is ineffective. The COVID pandemic was painful, but when we look back we'll realize that God used it to eliminate things in our lives that weren't working. Some churches, for example, are realizing they were pouring tons of financial resources into programs or buildings that had no spiritual impact. Pruning revealed what is essential for us to make a powerful, Book of Acts–style impact on our communities.

Pruning brings new life and more fruit. A tree that has never been pruned looks good. But unless the dead wood is cut away along with the showy leaves, we will never see new blooms. The tree needs the knife—and so do we. The church will not look the same in the years to come. Right now we are an ugly sight, stripped of our big audiences, our celebrity preachers, and our cool worship bands. We have been reduced to basics. But with the cutting comes something fresh and powerful, something that is so much better than church as we knew it before.

Pruning draws us closer to Jesus. More than anything the knife brings us into a deeper connection with Jesus, the "true vine" (John 15:1). He promises that those who submit to His pruning process will abide closely with Him. Isn't this what we want? We cannot abide in Him if a thousand other things are distracting us. Life prior to the pandemic was too busy and too cluttered. Jesus wants our focus to be on Him. The process of pruning cuts away everything else so we can love Him and trust Him fully.

Ask the Lord to change you. Pray that He will make His priorities your priorities. Allow Him to perform divine surgery. Be willing to cut away anything that hinders your ability to make disciples for Jesus.

LET'S **PRAY** ABOUT IT

Lord, I want to bear much fruit for You. But I know that fruit comes only when we surrender to heaven's pruning process. I welcome Your pruning in my life. Cut away my unfruitful branches. You have permission to change my priorities and mess up my schedule. Help me to make discipleship my passion. And purify Your church so we can welcome a fresh movement of Your Holy Spirit.

ONE **FINAL** THOUGHT

Give me one hundred preachers who fear nothing but sin and desire nothing but God, and I care not a straw whether they be clergymen or laymen, such alone will shake the gates of hell and set up the kingdom of heaven upon earth.[5]

—JOHN WESLEY, REVIVALIST AND FOUNDER, METHODISM

DISCIPLESHIP TIP
You Have an Expiration Date

I hope I have many more years to serve God. But now that I'm in my sixties I've never been more aware of the brevity of life. We have only a short time on this earth to fulfill our God-given assignment. I know I have an expiration date—and that's the reason I'm so intentional about discipleship. Before I go to heaven I want to invest in as many people as possible for Jesus Christ.

The apostle Paul focused his life on making disciples. He told the Corinthians: "For this reason I have sent to you Timothy... and he will remind you of my ways" (1 Cor. 4:17). Wherever Paul sent his beloved spiritual son, Timothy carried the same heart and message as Paul. And after Paul died, Timothy continued his legacy. God can do the same through you! Don't let your gospel witness end with you. Be intentional. Invest your life in your Timothys so they will continue to spread Christ's love long after heaven's chariots have taken you to glory.

CHAPTER 11

It's Time to Get Out
of Your Boat!

IF YOU CHOOSE to follow Jesus, sooner or later He will ask
you to do something scary that requires more faith than you
think you can muster. That is a guarantee. Jesus loves to
stretch us. He never leaves us the way He finds us. No one knew
this better than the disciple Peter.

The simple fisherman from Galilee had been called Simon all
his life. He was just "Simon the son of John." But when Jesus met
him the Savior immediately changed his name. He gave His disciple a new identity when He said: "You shall be called Cephas"
(John 1:42).

Cephas is the Aramaic word for *rock*; Peter is the Greek word
for the same.[1] Jesus obviously saw something in Peter—something that Peter didn't see in himself. Jesus saw stability and
strength. He saw a commanding leader. He was basically saying
to Peter: "Follow Me and you will discover who you really are. I
am going to use you. I am going to make you a great influencer."

From that day Peter stepped into a wonderful yet terrifying
process. By following Jesus, he gave the Master permission to
shape the humble clay of his life. Peter was probably aware of his
flaws—he was impatient, impulsive, too quick to open his mouth,
and sometimes too self-confident. Peter also was swayed by the

opinions of people, and this weakness led him to deny the Lord. But Jesus saw the potential in Peter from the beginning, and He was willing to put up with his flaws. He knew what Peter would eventually become.

All Jesus needed Peter to have was a willing heart.

Of all the strenuous leadership lessons Peter learned during his training process, his experience in the boat on the Sea of Galilee must have been the most harrowing. We tend to forget that when Jesus called Peter to walk on water, it was during the fourth watch of the night, which is between 3:00 and 6:00 a.m.

Seriously? If Jesus ever called me to walk on water, I'd prefer that the lesson be in broad daylight on a calm lake. Storms are bad enough, but storms in the dark of night with lightning, thunder, violent winds, and choppy waves? Yet it was in that turbulent setting that Jesus appeared on the sea and called to Peter, "Come!" (Matt. 14:29).

It's obvious Jesus was not making it easy for Peter; He designed this strenuous training exercise to enlarge Peter's faith. Don't expect that Jesus will make it comfortable for you either. Jesus allows tests and trials so we will grow. He structures our training process, as He did Peter's:

> Peter said to Him, "Lord, if it is You, command me to come to you on the water." And He said, "Come!" And Peter got out of the boat, and walked on the water and came toward Jesus. But seeing the wind, he became frightened, and beginning to sink, he cried out, "Lord, save me!" Immediately Jesus stretched out His hand and took hold of him, and said to him, "You of little faith, why did you doubt?" When they got into the boat, the wind stopped.
>
> —MATTHEW 14:28–32

When we read this story, we typically focus on Peter's failure to keep his eyes on Jesus or on the fact that he sank. But notice that after the crisis Jesus and Peter "got into the boat" (v. 32). Peter obviously walked on the swirling waves, even if he was holding on to his Teacher for dear life. He passed the test! His little faith had become bigger when he sat down with his friends on the boat. He was out of his comfort zone now, and he would learn to live more dangerously from that point on.

This is the challenge that faces every Christian. We would prefer to follow Jesus from the comfortable sidelines, but that is not the way of biblical discipleship. Jesus doesn't play it safe. He calls us to the center of the storm, and then He invites us to leave all that is secure. He calls us to an uncomfortable life.

It was evangelist Billy Graham who said: "Salvation is free, but discipleship costs everything we have." I hope you are ready to pay the full price.

Throughout this book I have shared how Jesus invites us to a life of maturity and fruitfulness. He invites us to grow spiritually so that we can help others mature spiritually. He wants us to invest in others so they can grow. But we cannot do this from the comfort of a padded seat. We must get up, step over the edge of the boat, and step onto the swirling waters. There are no shortcuts. If you are going to make disciples you must follow Peter's example.

Stop Disqualifying Yourself

My friend Jesse Laubach has been following the Lord faithfully for twenty-five years, and he and his wife, Jari, are raising two daughters to love Jesus. Jesse has been a fixture at Life Church in Allentown, Pennsylvania, since 1997, and he has served wherever needed—as an usher, a greeter, in the marriage ministry, and on the homeless outreach team.

But like so many Christians I know Jesse has stayed behind an invisible line in regard to certain leadership responsibilities. He especially doesn't like the microphone, even though people are blessed when he shares anything from the pulpit. He feels so insecure about public speaking that the thought of giving a sermon triggers intense anxiety.

God has also been calling Jesse to make disciples. He knows he's supposed to be making himself available to men who need direction, instruction, and fathering. That's one reason he reached out to me in 2021. He knew he needed additional mentoring in order to become a mentor. But of course Jesse feels more comfortable in his "boat."

I can relate to Jesse because I used to live in the shadows of insecurity and fear. God began calling me out of my comfortable hiding place back in 1998, and I wrestled with Him for months before surrendering.

I suspect He is calling you too.

When the Lord sent the prophet Samuel to anoint the next king of Israel, David was on the backside of the family farm. He was not even invited to greet Samuel. Apparently David's father, Jesse, and the others there did not count David worthy to be considered for this job interview. But after Samuel met seven of David's brothers, the Lord said through Samuel, "The LORD has not chosen these" (1 Sam. 16:10).

When Samuel asked if there were any more candidates, Jesse admitted he had one other son, the youngest, who was busy tending sheep. David was awkwardly presented to the prophet as an afterthought. But when Samuel poured the oil on him and "the Spirit of the LORD came mightily upon David" (v. 13), the unqualified suddenly became a warrior.

Whenever I pray over the global church in this season I see a massive crowd of people on the edge of a battlefield. Some are awkwardly wearing battle armor; others are sitting down on benches; all are avoiding the spotlight. This crowd represents the reluctant warriors God wants to use. They know they are called, but their feelings of insecurity, disqualification, and fear have paralyzed them. They know God wants to use them to train other warriors and make disciples. But they are stuck in a valley of shadows.

I hear the Holy Spirit saying this: "Now is the time for My reluctant warriors to surrender. Strip off the labels of failure you have been wearing. Stop listening to the accusations of the enemy. I have not disqualified you! Put on your armor and take your positions in battle. I am mobilizing My army, and I need My timid soldiers to come out of hiding."

If you are one of these reluctant recruits, I invite you to make a powerful decision. You have been stuck in limbo, but God can deliver you from your paralysis. I would advise you to take a posture of surrender—get on your knees, lift your hands, and tell God that you will do whatever He says, go wherever He commands you to go, and say whatever He tells you to say.

Your prayer should be "not my will, but Yours be done" (Luke 22:42). Then take these three steps:

1. Surrender your fears. Whether it's a fear of public speaking, a fear of leading a small group, a fear of social interaction, or a fear of criticism, renounce your fears in Jesus' name. Second Timothy 1:7 says: "For God has not given us a spirit of timidity, but of power and love and discipline." Don't wait for the butterflies to go away or your palms to stop sweating. You'll never break free until you actually step out and do what you fear. Goliath may look intimidating, but the truth is he is afraid of us because God is on our side.

2. Surrender your comforts. Many people have become complacent in this season, partly due to the COVID-19 quarantine. Life is easier when we are cocooned inside our homes, watching TV in our pajamas, and hiding from the stresses of life. But God didn't create us for selfish isolation. Whether you feel like it or not, venture out. It will feel very awkward when you first get out of your boat, but if you keep your eyes on Jesus instead of on the waves, you will learn to walk in a new way.

3. Surrender your plans. Too many of us have settled for less. We've boxed ourselves in to the ordinary and predictable. Be willing to set aside what you thought was best and ask God to reveal His big dreams for you. Simply pray: "Lord, don't let me live a status quo life. I yield to Your plans, no matter how much bigger they are than my own."

If You Want God to Use You, Open Your Valves

A few years ago the Lord challenged me about my level of spiritual hunger. He showed me that even though I had repeatedly sung the words, "Lord, I want more of You," I wasn't as passionate for Him as I thought I was.

In 1999 my church sponsored a conference on the Holy Spirit. At the close of one service I was lying on the floor near the altar asking God for another touch of His power. Several other people were kneeling at the communion rail and praying quietly for each other.

Suddenly I had a vision. In my mind I could see a large pipeline, at least eight feet in diameter. I was looking at it from the inside, and I could see a shallow stream of golden liquid flowing at the bottom. The oil in the giant pipe was only a few inches deep. I began a conversation with the Lord.

"What are You showing me?" I asked.

"I'm showing you a picture of the flow of the Holy Spirit in your life," He answered.

It was not an encouraging picture; it was pitiful! The capacity of the pipeline was huge—enough to convey a gushing river of oil. Yet only a trickle was evident. Then I noticed something else: several large valves were lined up along the sides of the pipeline, and each of them was shut.

I wanted to ask the Lord why there was so little oil in my life. Instead I asked, "What are those valves, and why are they closed?"

His answer stunned me. "Those represent the times when you said no. Why should I increase the level of anointing if you aren't available to use it?"

The words stung. When had I said no to God? I was overcome with emotion and began to repent. Then I recalled different excuses I had made and limitations I had placed on how He could use me.

I had told God that I didn't want to be in front of crowds because I wasn't a good speaker. I had told Him that if I couldn't preach like a famous TV minister, I didn't want to speak at all. I had told Him that I didn't want to address certain issues or go certain places. I had put so many conditions on my obedience!

After a while I began to see something else in my spirit. It was a huge crowd of African people, assembled in a large arena. And I saw myself preaching to them.

Nobody had ever asked me to minister in Africa, but I knew at that moment I needed to surrender my stubborn will. All I could think to say was the prayer of Isaiah: "Here am I. Send me!" (See Isaiah 6:8.) I told God I would go anywhere and say anything He asked. I laid my insecurities, fears, and inhibitions on the altar.

Three years later I stood behind a pulpit inside a sports arena in Port Harcourt, Nigeria. As I addressed a crowd of eight thousand pastors who had assembled there for a training conference, I remembered seeing their faces in that vision. And I realized that God had opened a new valve in my life that day in 1999. Because I had said yes He increased the flow of His oil so that it could reach thousands.

Many of us have a habit of asking for more of God's power and anointing. But what do we use it for? He doesn't send it just to make us feel good.

We love to go to the altar for a touch from God. We love the goose bumps, the shaking, and all the emotions of the moment. We love to fall on the floor and experience one infilling of the Holy Spirit after another. But I'm afraid some of us are soaking up the anointing and not giving it away. Our experience with the Holy Spirit has become inward and selfish. We just get up off the floor and live as we want to.

If we truly want to be empowered, we must offer God an unqualified yes. We must crucify every no. We must become a conduit to reach others, not a reservoir with no outlet. Search your heart and see whether there are any closed valves in your pipeline. As you surrender them, the locked channels will open and His oil will flow out to a world that craves to know He is real. It is only through this depth of surrender that you can become a disciple maker.

Are You One of God's Gideons?

During one of the darkest times in ancient Israel, Midianite invaders began a campaign of terror. God's people were hiding in caves and mountain strongholds. They had seen the Lord do miracles in the past to deliver Israel, but this time they lost all faith. (See Judges 6:1–6.)

But then the angel of the Lord visited a frightened young man named Gideon, who was hiding in a winepress. Gideon assumed God had given up on Israel. I'm sure he was shocked when the angel greeted him by saying, "The LORD is with you, O mighty man of valor" (Judg. 6:12, MEV). He thought the angel was talking to the wrong person.

"*Warrior?* You're talking to *me*?"

Gideon felt like a wimp. Yet the angel announced that God had recruited Gideon to be a deliverer for the nation—and Gideon wasn't having it! He gave the angel several reasons why he wasn't qualified. "How shall I deliver Israel?" Gideon asked. "Behold, my family is the least in Manasseh, and I am the youngest in my father's house" (Judg. 6:15).

Gideon was trying to become history's first draft dodger. But the Lord ignored each of his lame excuses. Finally, after a series of dramatic confirmations—including fire from heaven—Gideon suited up and headed to the battle. And he and his small band of three hundred soldiers supernaturally defeated the Midianite hordes. The story proves that one person who trusts God is more powerful than the majority. (See Judges 6:15–7:25.)

Like Gideon, many Christians are in hiding. They attend church. They listen to sermons. They sing worship songs along with everyone else in the congregation. But in their hearts they have gone AWOL when it comes to actively engaging in ministry.

They are timid spectators, waiting for someone else to act. They have disengaged. They don't believe God can use them.

Like Gideon, they have a list of excuses: "I've made too many mistakes." "I'm too old." "I'm too young." "My family is a mess." "I'm divorced." "I don't have any training." "I struggle with addictions." "I have too many doubts and hang-ups." "I think God is disappointed with me." Blah, blah, blah. Does any of this sound familiar to you?

I believe the Holy Spirit wants to interrupt all negative self-talk. He is saying, "I am calling all Gideons out of their hiding places!" This is the time for the weak to say, "I am strong." This is the time for spectators to get back in the game. We are heading into a fierce spiritual conflict, and we need all hands on deck!

Gideon's story is in the Bible because every one of us is like him. We struggle to believe that God wants to use us to carry His message and His power to a broken world. We are all tempted to hide in our caves.

Yet God puts His Holy Spirit in imperfect vessels. The apostle Paul told the Corinthians, "But we have this treasure in earthen vessels, so that the surpassing greatness of the power will be of God and not from ourselves" (2 Cor. 4:7). If you have been in hiding, crawl out of your cave and take these important steps:

Let go of your shame. Many Christians don't believe Jesus has forgiven them fully for their past sins. The devil loves to replay our sins over and over so we will wallow in condemnation. You must believe God's Word and renounce the devil's lies. Your sins have been washed away, and you have been made righteous.

Swallow your fears. Fear can paralyze. It will stop you from ever taking a risk. Yet the Bible promises: "God has not given us the spirit of fear" (2 Tim. 1:7, MEV). Gideon started out as a fearful man, but in the end he became a champion. You can experience the same transformation.

Stop disqualifying yourself. I have met so many followers of Christ who think they are not really on the team. They hide in the shadows, take the back seats in church, and never volunteer to do anything because they see themselves as misfits. Don't you realize God loves to take failures and make them successful? If He can restore Peter—who denied Him three times—and make him an apostle, He can redeem your past mistakes.

Don't compare. Most of my life I've struggled with inferiority. I compared myself with other men and felt as if I didn't measure up—either because of wealth, success, physique, or athletic ability. Then when I began to do ministry I compared myself with other preachers. They seemed more popular. Their preaching seemed more anointed than mine. Comparison is depressing.

But God makes each of us unique, and I must accept who I am. Psalm 139:14 says, "I am fearfully and wonderfully made." I don't have to preach like T. D. Jakes or Steven Furtick. God made me to be me! Paul said every Christian is uniquely gifted. He wrote, "If the foot says, 'Because I am not a hand, I am not a part of the body,' it is not for this reason any the less a part of the body" (1 Cor. 12:15).

Don't covet other people's gifts, and don't belittle your own. Enjoy how God made you, and celebrate the gifts of others. Most of all, be obedient to use your gifts to advance God's kingdom.

Tear off every label. So many of us have been programmed for defeat by our past experiences. Friends, teachers, bosses, or family members may have belittled you. Bullies may have told you that you are stupid, ugly, irresponsible, or useless. But those people do not have the ultimate power to define you. Let God heal you of those wounds.

Embrace your new identity. After Gideon had done what God directed him to do, his father gave him a new name. He was called Jerubbaal, which means, "Let Baal contend against him" (Judg. 6:32). The name clearly meant that Gideon became a serious threat after he struck down the false god Baal. The wimp had become a warrior!

Please stop hiding in the shadows. The alarm has sounded. Like Peter, you need to get out of your boat. Like Gideon, you need to suit up and run to the battle. God can use only those who have surrendered fully to His invitation. Please take a moment now to surrender to His call on your life.

LET'S **PRAY** ABOUT IT

Lord, You have called every Christian to make disciples. It feels like an overwhelming task, but I choose today to obey You. As Peter did, I choose to step out of my boat and follow You, even if it feels impossible and frightening. Give me Your supernatural boldness. I don't want to live a comfortable, status quo life. I would rather be with You on the scary waves. I choose to walk with You on the water. Amen.

ONE **FINAL** THOUGHT

If you feel weak, limited, ordinary, you are the best material through which God can work.[2]

—HENRY BLACKABY, COAUTHOR, *EXPERIENCING GOD*

DISCIPLESHIP TIP
You Need Total Surrender

As I mentioned previously, Jesus did four things when He fed the five thousand. (See Mark 6:33–44.) First, He *took* the bread and the fish; second, He *blessed* the food; third, He *broke* the food; and fourth, He *gave* the food to the multitude. This is how God works with us. He *takes* us, He *blesses* us, He *breaks* us, and then He gives His life through us to others.

If you want to be used by God, you cannot skip the third step. We love to be blessed, but few of us want to be broken. If you have not been broken you cannot reach your full potential to impact others around you. Your influence will be determined by how much you allow the brokenness of God in your life. Submit to His dealings. Yield to His plan. If you fully embrace His will in total surrender, your life will feed a multitude.

CHAPTER 12

Don't Try This Without the Holy Spirit!

O F ALL THE places I visited during my 2018 trip to Israel, my favorite was Jacob's well, the spot where Jesus ministered to the Samaritan woman. The authenticity of many sites in the Holy Land is disputed, but there is no question about this famous well, which is located in the modern city of Nablus in the West Bank.[1]

Now housed inside a Greek Orthodox church, the well is carved into solid rock. Visitors are allowed to lower a container down into the well, bring up water, and drink it. I was fascinated by how long it took to retrieve the water. And when I poured some of it back into the well, I waited several seconds to hear a faint splash. This well is 131 feet deep—about as deep as a nine-story building is tall!

I was in awe. Jesus actually sat in the same spot where I was standing. And that was where He told the woman of Samaria: "Everyone who drinks of this water will thirst again; but whoever drinks of the water that I will give him shall never thirst; but the water that I will give him will become in him a well of water springing up to eternal life" (John 4:13–14).

Jesus sat next to a deep well that represented the faith of the Jewish patriarchs. Yet He told this woman that there was something more. Something better. Something deeper than she had ever imagined. Jacob's well was incredibly deep, but Jesus calls us so much deeper. He was inviting the Samaritan woman to find Him, the one and only Savior of the world. His words made her thirstier and thirstier, and her decision to believe in the Messiah resulted in an entire village embracing faith in Him. (See John 4:10–15, 28–30, 39.)

Jesus' encounter with that woman reminds us how He wants to use us in His plan of redemption. He looked into that unnamed woman's eyes and saw all the pain she had endured. She had lived through five difficult marriages. She was most likely an outcast in her village because of her unspecified problems. She was living with a man who was not her husband, and she probably hid behind her veil every day because of her shame. (See John 4:16–18.)

But when she met Jesus He removed the weight of her burden. She felt free for the first time in her life. Jesus looked into the darkness of her pain and told her everything she ever did (John 4:29), and yet she did not feel condemned. She was liberated. She felt forgiven. That's why she ran into the village and announced to everyone that the Messiah had come (v. 28).

A broken woman with an ugly past had a chance encounter with the Savior, and before the day was over she became a bold evangelist. Jesus transformed her! She got a taste of the cool, refreshing water that flows from His heart, and she shared it with others.

You may never visit Jacob's well in Israel, but He is calling you to explore the depths of who He is. He is asking you to leave the shallowness of superficial Christianity. Regardless of what you have experienced, He offers more. He beckons all of us to go deeper.

The apostle Paul experienced miracles, received help from angels, heard the audible voice of Jesus, and saw visions of the third heaven. (See Acts 9:4–5, 18; 27:23–24; and 2 Corinthians 12:2.) Yet he wrote of "the unfathomable riches of Christ" in Ephesians 3:8. The Greek word for *unfathomable* can also mean "untraceable," "past finding out," or "unsearchable."[2]

Paul used this same imagery when he prayed that the Ephesians would be able to comprehend "what is the breadth and length and height and depth, and to know the love of Christ which surpasses knowledge, that you may be filled up to all the fullness of God" (Eph. 3:18–19).

Do you desire to experience this fullness? Do you want to increase your capacity to know Christ? Or are you satisfied to stay where you are? I encourage you to let God call you to the depths.

I relate to the psalmist who wrote, "My soul thirsts for God, for the living God" (Ps. 42:2). As his passion intensified, he continued: "Deep calls to deep at the noise of Your waterfalls; all Your waves and Your billows passed over me" (v. 7, MEV). When we choose to go deeper, the journey will become more intense. Spiritual growth is not easy. We must press through all resistance. We must let go of our apathy and selfishness.

How much labor was required for Jacob and his sons to bore a well 131 feet deep into solid rock? I don't know how many years or how much sweat was required, but I know the water didn't spring up overnight. Salvation is free, but a deep relationship with Christ takes time—and many Christians give up and settle for a mediocre experience.

God is waiting for a response from you. Jesus didn't call Peter to walk on water until Peter first asked for the miracle. Peter said: "Lord, if it is You, bid me come to You on the water" (Matt. 14:28, MEV). Only then did Jesus say, "Come!" (v. 29).

Jesus wants you to walk on the waves with Him. He invites us all to experience a miraculous adventure of faith. He wants you to become a disciple maker so that you can multiply His life in others. But He waits for you to desire this multiplied life.

The prophet Ezekiel saw a vision of a spiritual river that flowed eastward from the temple in Jerusalem. (See Ezekiel 47:1–2.) The water began as a trickle from the south side of the building, but as it flowed out it became deeper and deeper. An angel measured the water as it went from ankle-deep to knee-deep to waist-deep

(vv. 3–4). Then it became a wide, expansive river—"a river that could not be forded" (v. 5).

Ezekiel's vision reminds us that there are different levels in God. We experience the shallow water when we first embrace faith in Jesus. But He does not want us to spend our whole lives in the baby pool. He calls us to be discipled, to grow in prayer and other spiritual disciplines, and to learn to trust Him. Then He invites us to go even deeper, until our feet cannot touch the bottom and we allow His strong current to take us where He wants us.

This book has been calling you to the deepest part of God's river. Only those who venture into the depths will be used to influence others for Jesus. Disciple makers do not just kick and splash in the shallow end or lie on the beach watching the fishing boats pass by. Disciple makers get swept up in the raging current and go wherever God takes them.

Many decades ago revivalist A. W. Tozer challenged Christians to stoke the fires of spiritual passion. He wrote, "Complacency is a deadly foe of all spiritual growth. Acute desire must be present or there will be no manifestation of Christ to His people. He waits to be wanted. Too bad that with many of us He waits so long, so very long, in vain."[3]

I wonder what Tozer would think if he saw our level of spiritual hunger today. Few believers today are willing to bore deep to discover the depths of God's "more." We are smug and satisfied. I dare you to get out of your boat and say to Jesus: "Bid me to come to You on the water." It is time for you to leave all complacency behind and begin drinking from the depths.

The brutal truth is that a large majority of Christians today will not read this book and have no interest in making disciples. For them, disciple making is for full-time pastors and those "special" Christians who go to church often. It is safe to say that 80 percent of Bible-believing, born-again Christians are just flat-out uninterested and unmotivated to lead others to Christ or to disciple them.

That means the 20 percent of highly engaged Christians has to work harder and be more committed. Thankfully we do not have to rely on our sweat to do the work. The Holy Spirit promises to empower us. Discipleship is His mission, so He is eager to give us the supernatural ability to do it.

Be Filled With the Holy Spirit

If you could go back in time and visit the tabernacle of Moses, one thing would immediately catch your attention. You would smell the strong fragrance of anointing oil. Everything inside the tent would have been dripping with this sweet-smelling compound, which was made of crushed cinnamon, myrrh, and other spices mixed with olive oil. (See Exodus 30:22–25.)

God told Moses to pour the anointing oil on everything in that holy place. The Lord said the tent itself should be anointed with oil, as well as the ark of the covenant, the table of showbread, the lampstand, the incense altar, the laver and its stand, the altar of burnt offering, and every utensil used during worship. (See Exodus 30:26–28.)

God also commanded Moses to anoint the priests (Exod. 30:30). It wasn't enough for the structure and all the furniture inside to be covered with the holy anointing oil. Anyone who was permitted to enter that sanctuary had to be anointed.

After Moses constructed the tabernacle, God sent fire from heaven to ignite the sacrifice (Lev. 9:24). And the Lord told Moses to keep the fire burning always (Lev. 6:9, 12–13). The same thing happened when Solomon's temple was built (2 Chron. 7:1). God sent a holy fire from heaven. Now, in the new covenant era, God's fire doesn't burn in buildings. He sends the fire of the Holy Spirit to blaze inside of us.

The church today should be the contemporary counterpart of the ancient tabernacle. In this age of the new covenant God wants His church to be dripping—not with physical oil but with the Holy Spirit's supernatural power!

That isn't what we see in most churches today. God told Moses

FOLLOW ME

to prepare the anointing oil in hefty, one-and-a-half-gallon containers.⁴ (See Exodus 30:22–24.) Today the tiny vials of oil we keep on our church altars are an accurate reflection of our low level of anointing. We have become satisfied with little or no oil. We are dry and powerless.

Theologian John Stott made it clear that we can't make disciples effectively in our own power and ability: "Without the Holy Spirit," Stott said, "Christian discipleship would be inconceivable, even impossible. There can be no life without the life giver, no understanding without the Spirit of truth, no fellowship without the unity of the Spirit, no Christlikeness of character apart from His fruit, and no effective witness without His power. As a body without breath is a corpse, so the church without the Spirit is dead."⁵

Ralph Vogel, a pastor friend in Pittsburgh, told me several years ago that he had been studying about the way Old Testament priests were anointed for service. He was intrigued by the fact that one of David's psalms makes reference to the holy anointing oil drizzling down the robes of God's ministers:

> Behold, how good and how pleasant it is for brothers to dwell together in unity! It is like the precious oil upon the head, coming down upon the beard, even Aaron's beard, coming down upon the edge of his robes.
> —PSALM 133:1–2

Obviously if the oil was dripping down Aaron's beard and oozing down to the hem of his garments, he was not being anointed with a few drops from a tiny vial. Ralph discovered that the fragrant oil was not used sparingly in ancient anointing services. The priests were literally slathered with oil, reminding us that we need an abundance of the Holy Spirit's power to do His work.

While I was with Ralph the weekend in Pittsburgh when he shared this revelation, he asked if I would like to experience this type of anointing ceremony. He had actually purchased several large containers of olive oil, and he offered to conduct an Old Testament–style anointing service just so I could understand how one might have been conducted in the days of Moses.

My disciple Dante and I both volunteered. We changed into shorts and T-shirts, and Pastor Ralph and some of his church members placed towels on the floor. Then Ralph prayed over us and poured almost a gallon of oil on us. We were saturated!

I don't believe everyone has to go through an experience like this. God can fill you with His Holy Spirit without using any oil from a vial or jug. But the lesson is clear: If you want God to use you, you must have the fullness of His power. You cannot rely on your own ability.

Ephesians 5:18 has been a life verse for me since I was filled with the Holy Spirit as a young man. It says: "And do not get drunk with wine, for that is dissipation, but be filled with the Spirit." God wants you to be filled to overflowing with His anointing. Why be dry when you can be saturated?

Paul told Timothy to "kindle afresh the gift of God which is in you through the laying on of my hands" (2 Tim. 1:6). Like Timothy, you must fuel the flames of personal devotion and keep your faith red hot. Never let anything quench it! As a mentor, you need more than a mediocre fire. Your life should be a raging bonfire. You must set your thermostat high so you can ignite others.

Don't be just a candle; be a blowtorch. Your level of anointing will determine the extent of your influence. You must guard your fire as if your life depends on it.

Pray for the Power

In the traditional Baptist church in which I grew up, we talked a lot about Jesus, but the Holy Spirit was rarely mentioned. There was a song in our hymnal called "Pentecostal Power," but we never sang it. I always wondered why.

The lack of emphasis on the Holy Spirit is a sad reality for many churches today. We don't preach about the Holy Spirit; we don't make room for the Holy Spirit's gifts or ministries. And in many churches leaders might as well stand at the front door to keep the Holy Spirit out. He is not welcome.

Even today in many churches that wear a "Spirit-filled" label, fewer and fewer people know what it means to be baptized in the Spirit. And in many nondenominational Bible churches the services are so tightly scripted and the sermons so geared for new believers that we rarely challenge believers to go deeper in their faith.

If your church welcomes the Holy Spirit and encourages people to be filled with His life and power, you are part of a wonderful new movement of God that is emerging in our generation. The best thing you can do is stay on fire and spread the flame to others.

I believe every church needs Pentecost. Not an annual celebration of an event in church history, but a living, breathing, awe-inspiring encounter with the Holy Spirit that shakes every church member to the core. To do church without Pentecost is actually unbiblical. To go for year after year without the power of God is inexcusable. Any pastor who is content to go through the motions of church without the Holy Spirit's full involvement is not a good steward of the grace they were given when they accepted the call of God.

You may think those are strong words, but British preacher Charles Spurgeon said it more forcefully in the 1800s than I just did. He wrote: "The lack of distinctly recognizing the power of the Holy Ghost lies at the root of many useless ministries."[6] It is true. If we don't rely on the Holy Spirit's power and encourage people in our churches to experience His power, then church is useless. Why? Because the Holy Spirit is the One who empowers believers to live for God and reach the world for Christ!

There is a difference between *receiving* the Holy Spirit at conversion and *being baptized* in the Holy Spirit. I received the Holy Spirit at the moment I became a born-again Christian. The Spirit began to lead me. I felt His comfort when I was going through a test or trial. I started hearing His still, small voice.

But years later I learned that I needed to be filled, or baptized, with the Holy Spirit for the purpose of empowerment. For me, it was a second experience. Sadly, many, many Christians go through their entire lives without availing themselves of this vital resource because so many churches do not emphasize the need for the Holy Spirit's power. We have invented a weak version of Christianity that is devoid of Pentecost.

When you are filled with the Spirit, you begin to walk in a greater dimension of His power. You may begin to see visions and dreams. God may release in you the gifts of prophecy, healing, or speaking in tongues. In the past some churches tried to restrict these gifts, thinking that people who claimed to have spiritual gifts were fanatics. But it is becoming more obvious every day that the church needs the fullness of the Holy Spirit's power if we are going to reach this wayward world. We need to walk in the same power that the church experienced in the Book of Acts.

I received the baptism of the Holy Spirit when I was eighteen, just before going to college. My life was transformed by that experience. And since then I have prayed for countless people to have the same anointing. I have reminded them that they don't have to rely on a tiny vial of oil—they have a giant vat of the Holy Spirit's power.

Some people receive the baptism of the Holy Spirit immediately when I pray for them. Others seem to take more time. It may be a process for you. But I have also discovered that some people don't receive because they have blockages in their lives that prevent the Spirit from flowing in fullness. Some people struggle with doubt or intellectual pride; others are bound by religious traditions; some are actually afraid of the Holy Spirit's miracles; and some are hindered by hidden sins they have never confessed. But I have found that one of the most common hindrances to being filled with the Holy Spirit is an unyielded attitude.

You cannot be filled with the Holy Spirit if you are full of yourself. Some people are too willful. They have not surrendered their plans, finances, relationships, or time to God. They have their lives planned out, and they don't want God interrupting their agendas. Yet God is looking to fill hearts that have been emptied and surrendered. Only the fully yielded can experience the fullness of His power.

When Jesus called His first followers, He didn't make it easy for them. He drew a line in the sand. He made it clear that discipleship is not for the indifferent window-shopper or the casual inquirer. To follow Christ demands a decision; it requires full surrender. It demands repentance from sin, total consecration to God, and a willingness to lay down one's life even unto death. Jesus said, "If anyone wishes to come after Me, he must deny himself, and take up his cross and follow Me" (Matt. 16:24). German theologian Dietrich Bonhoeffer said it this way: "When Christ calls a man, he bids him come and die."[7]

This book is your invitation to surrender your life fully to a life of service. God wants all His followers to invest their lives in others—and we can do this only by emptying ourselves and asking His Holy Spirit to fill us and then pour out of us. Do you want to be His vessel? Do you want to make disciples? Lift your hands and surrender right now to the call.

Jesus gave us His mandate, what we call the Great Commission, just before He ascended to the Father. He said: "Go therefore and make disciples of all the nations, baptizing them in the name of the Father and the Son and the Holy Spirit, teaching them to observe all that I commanded you; and lo, I am with you always, even to the end of the age" (Matt. 28:19–20).

The Great Commission was not a suggestion. Jesus was not inviting us to debate over His words or vote on whether we should take them seriously. Jesus was giving us marching orders. He expected obedience from His first-century followers, and He expects the same obedience from us today.

Don't resist. Don't make up excuses. Don't look for an escape hatch. Don't squirm on the altar. Don't kid yourself, thinking that a life of making disciples is for only those in full-time ministry. If you are a follower of Jesus, He has already demanded all your time. He has called you to deny yourself and die to your own ambitions, plans, and dreams.

Just say yes to the call of God. When you are fully surrendered, it will be easy for you to be filled with the Holy Spirit. He loves to fill empty vessels. He will empower you for this adventure. He will drench you with His oil.

Prepare for your own personal Pentecost. God wants to pour the anointing oil on you until you are fully saturated so the life of Jesus can overflow into the lives of many others. He has done this for me. I know He will do it for you.

LET'S **PRAY** ABOUT IT

Lord, so many Christians are content to experience only Your benefits and blessings. But I don't want to live in the shallow end of Your river. I don't want to be a selfish follower of Christ. I want to share Your blessings. I want to be a conduit of Your love. Fill me with Your Holy Spirit so that Your power will overflow from me to the people around me. Baptize me in the Holy Spirit so I can be a bold witness. Amen.

ONE **FINAL** THOUGHT

Trying to do the Lord's work in your own strength is the most confusing, exhausting and tedious of all work. But when you are filled with the Holy Spirit, then the ministry of Jesus just flows out of you.[8]

—CORRIE TEN BOOM, DUTCH EVANGELIST

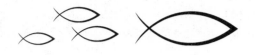

APPENDIX

Renew Your Mind
With God's Word

Scriptures to Renew Your Mind
About Your Identity in Christ

GIDEON WAS A timid man who struggled with inferiority. But the angel of the Lord came to him and said: "God is with you, O mighty warrior" (Judg. 6:12, MSG). Gideon didn't believe those words. He saw himself as a failure. But eventually he became a champion. He was transformed from a wimp to a warrior by believing what God said about him!

God wants to change the way you see yourself. Life may have programmed you to think you are a failure, stupid, weak, inferior, disqualified, or unlovable. Yet there are so many scriptures that describe your true identity. You will be transformed as you meditate on what God says about you. Meditate on these Bible verses daily so you can overcome the lies you have believed about yourself.

I am loved. Jeremiah 31:3 says: "I have loved you with an everlasting love; I have drawn you with unfailing kindness" (NIV). God's love for me is so great it is difficult to fathom. It will take all of eternity to fully comprehend how great His love is. In spite of my mistakes, my weaknesses, and my sins, God is kind and merciful, and He loves me unconditionally.

I am a child of God. My Father delights in me as a son or daughter. He is not angry with me. My loving Father accepts me and celebrates me. Ephesians 1:6 says, "He made us accepted in the Beloved" (NKJV). I am welcome in my Father's house!

I am forgiven. I have been washed in the blood of Christ. I am clean. He does not keep a file on my sins. He has purged everything from my record. He even chose to forget my sins! Ephesians 1:7 says, "We have redemption through His blood, the forgiveness of sins, according to the riches of His grace" (NKJV).

I am blameless. When God looks at me, He sees the righteousness of Jesus, not my sin. He took my filthy garments and gave me a new robe of righteousness. Ephesians 1:4 says He chose us before the foundation of the world, "that we would be holy and blameless before Him."

I have been adopted. The Father wanted me in His family. He paid the ultimate price so I could be His child. He drew me from far away so I could live with Him forever. I belong to Him! Romans 8:15 says I have "received a spirit of adoption...by which we cry out, 'Abba! Father!'" I can call God my Daddy!

I am an heir with Christ. I have a spiritual inheritance. Everything that belongs to the Father has been given to me. God does not withhold His goodness from me. Romans 8:17 says I am an heir of God and a fellow heir with Christ. Ephesians 1:3 says we have been blessed with every spiritual blessing in Christ.

I am free from sin. Sin doesn't have power over me. I can flee from temptation. Romans 6:18 says I am now a "slave of righteousness" because I've been freed from my past sins and addictions. Second Corinthians 5:17 says if anyone is in Christ, the old things have passed away and "all things have become new" (NKJV).

I am victorious. I am not just a conqueror. Romans 8:37 says we are "more than conquerors" because of Him who loved us.

Because of the victory that Christ won on the cross for me, I have also overcome sin and death. First John 4:4 says, "Greater is He who is in you than he who is in the world." The devil has been defeated!

I am the temple of the Holy Spirit. God's Holy Spirit lives in me, according to 1 Corinthians 6:19. I am never alone. God's presence is always with me because His Holy Spirit abides in me forever. And Jesus promised He will never leave me nor forsake me. He will never take His Holy Spirit from me.

I have received power. I've been filled with the Holy Spirit. Now I can lay hands on the sick and see them healed. I can cast out demons. I have authority over all the devil's power. Jesus said in Luke 10:19, "I have given you authority to tread on serpents and scorpions, and over all the power of the enemy."

I am a spiritual warrior. I wear the armor of God. I have the shield of faith, the helmet of salvation, and the sword of the Spirit. The devil will not be able to defeat me. Ephesians 6:10 says I am strong in the Lord and in the strength of His might! Even when I feel weak, I am strong because the Holy Spirit empowers me.

I have the peace of God. I will not be shaken by worry, fear, or anxiety. God comforts me and calms my fears. Philippians 4:7 says the peace of God, which surpasses all comprehension, will guard my heart and mind in Christ Jesus. I am not controlled by fear. Psalm 118:6 says, "The LORD is for me; I will not fear."

I am guided by God's Spirit. The Lord is my shepherd, and He leads me and guides me. I can hear His still, gentle voice. Psalm 32:8 promises me, "I will instruct you and teach you in the way which you should go." God directs my steps, gives me wisdom, and helps me make the right choices.

I am full of God's joy. My joy is not based on my circumstances. I can rejoice no matter what is going on in my life. When I feel discouraged, Nehemiah 8:10 promises, "The joy of the LORD is your strength." Even when I go through hard times, I know the pain will not last forever. I have the promise of Psalm 30:5: "Weeping may last for the night, but a shout of joy comes in the morning."

I am an ambassador for Christ. I can reconcile others to Jesus Christ. Everywhere I go people will be drawn to Jesus. Second Corinthians 5:20 says God has made me an ambassador. And 2 Corinthians 3:6 says God has made me an adequate minister of the new covenant. I am qualified not because of my own abilities but because God has qualified me.

I am God's masterpiece. God created me for a special purpose. He will use me to do good works that will bring glory to the Father. Ephesians 2:10 says I am God's "workmanship"— which means masterpiece. I am on a divine assignment, and I will fulfill God's mission for my life!

I am blessed. God sees me and cares for me. He is a good Father. He provides for my daily needs. Luke 6:38 says when I give to others, God will give to me "pressed down, shaken together, and running over." I will experience His supernatural provision. And Philippians 4:19 says my God supplies all of my need according to His riches in glory by Christ Jesus.

I am growing as a disciple. I am growing more stable every day because Jesus is my foundation. When I feel weak, confused, unstable, or tormented, I will find peace and stability in Christ, who is my refuge. Colossians 2:7 says I am "firmly rooted...built up...and established in [my] faith." Because I have strong roots in Christ, I will bear much fruit for God.

I always have access to His grace. Jesus has given me strength for every trial I face. He promises me in 2 Corinthians 12:9, "My grace is sufficient for you, for power is perfected in weakness." There will always be enough strength to face each day, no matter how weak I feel. God's grace will never run out!

I will live forever with Christ. Romans 6:23 says, "The free gift of God is eternal life in Christ Jesus our Lord." I will spend eternity in the presence of God. Revelation 21:27 says my name has been written in the Lamb's book of life; therefore I will dwell in the heavenly city with Christ when this life is over.

Notes

AUTHOR'S NOTE

1. Blue Letter Bible, s.v. "*ichthýs*," accessed June 29, 2021, https://www.blueletterbible.org/lexicon/g2486/kjv/tr/0-1/; Greg B. Dill, "The History of the Ichthus," Plymouth Church of Christ, accessed September 17, 2021, http://www.plymouth-church.com/ichthus.html.
2. New World Encyclopedia, s.v. "*Ichthys*," accessed September 17, 2021, https://www.newworldencyclopedia.org/entry/ichthys; Dill, "The History of the Ichthus."
3. Dill, "The History of the Ichthus"; New World Encyclopedia, s.v. "*Ichthys*."

CHAPTER 1

1. Ken Albert, Susan Fletcher, and Doug Hankins, eds., *Dawson Trotman: In His Own Words* (Colorado Springs, CO: NavPress, 2011), 205.

CHAPTER 2

1. Blue Letter Bible, s.v. "*typos*," accessed June 29, 2021, https://www.blueletterbible.org/lexicon/g5179/kjv/tr/0-1/.
2. Michael Safi, "Why Kumbh Mela in Prayagraj Is Festival to End All Festivals," *The Guardian*, January 14, 2019, https://www.theguardian.com/world/2019/jan/15/why-kumbh-mela-in-prayahraj-is-festival-to-end-all-festivals.

FOLLOW ME

3. "Largest Free Rock Concert Attendance," Guinness World Records, accessed September 20, 2021, https://www. guinnessworldrecords.com/world-records/73085-largest-free-rock-concert-attendance.

4. Valeriya Safronova, "James Charles, From 'CoverBoy' to Canceled," *New York Times*, May 14, 2019, https://www. nytimes.com/2019/05/14/style/james-charles-makeup-artist-youtube.html.

5. Ira M. Price, "The Schools of the Sons of the Prophets," *The Old Testament Student* 8, no. 7 (March 1889): 245–246, https://www.jstor.org/stable/3156528?seq=1#metadata_info_tab_contents. This article lists the schools at Ramah, Bethel, Gilgal, Jericho, Carmel, and Samaria.

6. During his ministry, Elijah performed eight miracles by the power of the Holy Spirit. At his death, Elisha had worked only fifteen miracles—one short of double. It would appear that the promise of God had come up short, but we know that this cannot be. God always keeps His word, even if it requires the most incredible display of power. Elisha had died and his body was laid in a sepulcher. Soon afterward, an invading army of Moabites came to Israel and passed near Elisha's grave. When one of the Moabite soldiers died, his fellow soldier threw his body into Elisha's sepulcher, and the corpse made contact with Elisha's bones. The recently fallen Moabite was resurrected and stood up on his feet. Thus, Elisha ultimately worked sixteen miracles, twice the number of his mentor.

7. Walter A. Henrichsen, *Disciples Are Made Not Born* (Wheaton, IL: Victor Books, 1981), 147–148.

8. "Born to Reproduce: Dawson Trotman," Discipleship Library, accessed October 11, 2021, http://turret2.discipleshiplibrary. com/AA094.mp3, https://www.nobts.edu/discipleship/

206

downloadable-documents1/spiritual-formation-folder/
Born%20to%20reproduce%20Dawson%20Trotman.pdf.

9. Henrichsen, *Disciples Are Made Not Born*, 141.
10. C. H. Spurgeon, "Wanted, A Guest Chamber!," sermon, Metropolitan Tabernacle, December 15, 1867, Spurgeon's Sermons, https://www.ccel.org/ccel/spurgeon/sermons13.lviii.html.

CHAPTER 3

1. Blue Letter Bible, s.v. "*agapētos*," accessed June 30, 2021, https://www.blueletterbible.org/lexicon/g27/kjv/tr/0-1/.
2. Ellie Cambridge, "Who Is Nikolas Cruz, Where Is the Parkland School Shooting Suspect Now, and When Will His Trial End?," *The Sun*, February 14, 2019, https://www.thesun.co.uk/news/5582904/nikolas-cruz-florida-shooting-marjory-stoneman-douglas-trial-rifle/.
3. Joel Rose, "Parkland Shooting Suspect: A Story of Red Flags, Ignored," NPR, March 1, 2018, https://www.npr.org/2018/02/28/589502906/a-clearer-picture-of-parkland-shooting-suspect-comes-into-focus.
4. Erin Calabrese and Elisha Fieldstadt, "Charleston Church Shooter Dylann Roof Was Loner Caught in 'Internet Evil': Family," NBC News, June 20, 2015, https://www.nbcnews.com/storyline/charleston-church-shooting/relatives-charleston-church-shooter-dylann-roof-describe-quiet-sweet-kid-n379071; Rachel Kaadzi Ghansah, "A Most American Terrorist: The Making of Dylann Roof," *Gentleman's Quarterly*, August 21, 2017, gq.com.
5. Edgar Sandoval, Chelsia Rose Marcius, and Ginger Adams Otis, "Orlando Shooter Was Regular at Pulse Gay Club; Former Classmate Says Omar Mateen Was Homosexual," *New York Daily News*, June 13, 2016, https://www.

nydailynews.com/news/national/orlando-shooter-reported-pulse-club-regular-patrons-article-1.2672445.

6. The Associated Press, "Victims of Pulse Nightclub Massacre Remembered 5 Years Later," ABC News, June 12, 2021, https://abcnews.go.com/US/wireStory/victims-pulse-nightclub-massacre-remembered-years-78245699.

7. Zusha Elinson, "One Year Later, Experts Dig Deeper to Find Vegas Shooter's Motive," *Wall Street Journal*, September 30, 2018, https://www.wsj.com/articles/one-year-later-experts-dig-deeper-to-find-vegas-shooters-motive-1538305200.

8. "Strong Relationships, Strong Health," Better Health Channel, accessed September 17, 2021, https://www.betterhealth.vic.gov.au/health/healthyliving/Strong-relationships-strong-health?viewAsPdf=true.

9. Christine Comaford, "Are You Getting Enough Hugs?" *Forbes*, August 22, 2020, https://www.forbes.com/sites/christinecomaford/2020/08/22/are-you-getting-enough-hugs/?sh=3ab12f9368da.

10. Jena McGregor, "This Former Surgeon General Says There's a 'Loneliness Epidemic' and Work Is Partly to Blame," *Washington Post*, October 4, 2017, https://www.washingtonpost.com/news/on-leadership/wp/2017/10/04/this-former-surgeon-general-says-theres-a-loneliness-epidemic-and-work-is-partly-to-blame/.

11. Jacqueline Olds, MD, and Richard S. Schwartz, MD, *The Lonely American: Drifting Apart in the Twenty-First Century* (Boston: Beacon Press, 2010), 58.

12. Blue Letter Bible, s.v. "*ektenōs*," accessed June 28, 2021, https://www.blueletterbible.org/lexicon/g1619/kjv/tr/0-1/.

13. Blue Letter Bible, s.v. "*koinōnia*," accessed June 30, 2021, https://www.blueletterbible.org/lexicon/g2842/kjv/tr/0-1/.

14. Blue Letter Bible, s.v. "*koinōnia.*"

15. Blue Letter Bible, s.v. "*dynamis,*" accessed June 30, 2021, https://www.blueletterbible.org/lexicon/g1411/kjv/tr/0-1/.

16. Charles Haddon Spurgeon, "The Queen of the South, or the Ernest Enquirer," sermon, Metropolitan Tabernacle, October 4, 1863, The Spurgeon Center, https://www. spurgeon.org/resource-library/sermons/the-queen-of-the-south-or-the-earnest-enquirer/#flipbook/.

17. C. H. Spurgeon, "Spurgeon's Maxims for Living: Friendship," Exploring the Mind and Heart of the Prince of Preachers, accessed June 30, 2021, http://www.spurgeon.us/mind_and_heart/quotes/f2.htm#friendship.

18. Nick McKeehan, "Loneliness and the Risk of Dementia," Cognitive Vitality, April 26, 2019, https://www.alzdiscovery. org/cognitive-vitality/blog/loneliness-and-the-risk-of-dementia.

19. Tom Carter, ed., *Spurgeon at His Best: Over 2200 Striking Quotations From the World's Most Exhaustive and Widely-Read Sermon Series* (Grand Rapids, MI: Baker, 1988), 72.

CHAPTER 4

1. Walter A. Henrichsen, *Thoughts From the Diary of a Desperate Man* (Colorado Springs, CO: Leadership Foundation, 2007), 63.

2. C. H. Spurgeon, "Friendship."

3. C. H. Spurgeon, "Others to Be Gathered In," sermon, Metropolitan Tabernacle, October 6, 1878, Spurgeon's Sermons, https://www.ccel.org/ccel/spurgeon/sermons24. xlvii.html.

4. C. S. Lewis, *The Four Loves* (New York: Harcourt Brace, 1960), 169–170.

Chapter 5

1. "Most Teenagers Drop Out of Church When They Become Young Adults," Lifeway Research, January 15, 2019, https://lifewayresearch.com/2019/01/15/most-teenagers-drop-out-of-church-as-young-adults/.

2. LeRoy Eims, *The Lost Art of Disciple Making* (Grand Rapids, MI: Zondervan, 1978), 45–46.

3. Blue Letter Bible, s.v. "*hāḡâ*," accessed September 17, 2021, https://www.blueletterbible.org/lexicon/h1897/kjv/wlc/0-1/.

4. Dale Reeves, "Chewing the Cud," Christ's Church, accessed September 17, 2021, https://ourchristschurch.com/chewing-the-cud/.

5. "Notes on Psalm 119" in *NASB Study Bible*, ed. Kenneth Barker (Grand Rapids, MI: Zondervan, 1999), 864.

6. Eric W. Hayden, "Charles H. Spurgeon: Did You Know?," Christian History Institute, accessed September 20, 2021, https://christianhistoryinstitute.org/magazine/article/spurgeon-did-you-know.

7. Charles H. Spurgeon, quoted in David Kakish, "Paul, His Cloak, and His Books," *Theology in the Middle*, February 5, 2015, https://theologyinthemiddle.com/thoughts/2015/02/05/paul-his-cloak-and-his-books.

8. Abarim Publications, s.v. "Ziklag," accessed September 17, 2021, https://www.abarim-publications.com/Meaning/Ziklag.html.

9. Blue Letter Bible, s.v. "*isopsychos*," accessed July 1, 2021, https://www.blueletterbible.org/lexicon/g2473/kjv/tr/0-1/.

10. Eims, *The Lost Art of Disciple Making, 72.*

Chapter 6

1. "Bear Bryant," AZ Quotes, accessed September 20, 2021, https://www.azquotes.com/quote/537649.

2. "Bear Bryant," BrainyQuote, accessed September 20, 2021, https://www.brainyquote.com/quotes/bear_bryant_381718.
3. Blue Letter Bible, s.v. "*agōn*," accessed July 2, 2021, https://www.blueletterbible.org/lexicon/g73/kjv/tr/0-1/; *Merriam-Webster*, s.v. "agony," accessed July 2, 2021, https://www.merriam-webster.com/dictionary/agony.
4. "World Child Hunger Facts," World Hunger Education Service, accessed September 17, 2021, https://www.worldhunger.org/world-child-hunger-facts/.
5. Howard Hendricks, quoted in Janet Renner Loyd, "Thinking of Spiritual Fathers," *A Branch in the Vine* (blog), June 13, 2013, https://www.abranchinthevine.com/blog/thinking-of-spiritual-fathers.

<h2 style="text-align:center">CHAPTER 7</h2>

1. "What Does John 6:7 Mean?" BibleRef.com, accessed July 8, 2021, https://www.bibleref.com/John/6/John-6-7.html#commentary.
2. Robert D. Foster, *The Navigator* (Colorado Springs, CO: NavPress, 1983), 78.
3. William Shakespeare, Act II, Scene 2 of *Romeo and Juliet*.
4. *Merriam-Webster*, s.v. "morrow," accessed October 6, 2021, https://www.merriam-webster.com/dictionary/morrow.
5. William Shakespeare, Act II, Scene 2 of *King Lear*.
6. *Merriam-Webster*, "7 Shakespearean Insults to Make Life More Interesting," September 16, 2021, https://www.merriam-webster.com/words-at-play/shakespeare-insults/hempen-homespun.
7. Blue Letter Bible, s.v. "*metadidōmi*," accessed July 2, 2021, https://www.blueletterbible.org/lexicon/g3330/kjv/tr/0-1/.
8. Vocabulary.com, s.v. "impart," accessed September 17, 2021, https://www.vocabulary.com/dictionary/impart.

9. Francis Chan with Mark Beuving, *Multiply: Disciples Making Disciples* (Colorado Springs, CO: David C. Cook, 2012), 36.

CHAPTER 8

1. Blue Letter Bible, s.v. *"ekdapanaō,"* accessed July 2, 2021, https://www.blueletterbible.org/search/dictionary/viewtopic.cfm?topic=VT0002729.

2. Erin E. Clack, "This Instagram Account Calls Out Celeb Church Pastors for Their Pricey Sneakers," FN, April 8, 2019, https://footwearnews.com/2019/focus/athletic-outdoor/preachers-n-sneakers-instagram-celebrity-pastors-fashion-1202769231/.

3. Henry and Richard Blackaby and Claude King, *Experiencing God* (Nashville, TN: B&H Publishing Group, 2008), 148.

4. Blue Letter Bible, s.v. *"epipiptō,"* accessed July 6, 2021, https://www.blueletterbible.org/lexicon/g1968/kjv/tr/0-1/.

5. John Stott, "Pride, Humility, and God," in *Alive to God*, ed. J. I. Packer and Loren Wilkinson (Downers Grove, IL: InterVarsity Press, 1992), 119.

CHAPTER 9

1. J. Warner Wallace, "The Brief Case for Peter's Influence on Mark's Gospel (Bible Insert)," Christianity.com, April 9, 2015, https://www.christianity.com/blogs/j-warner-wallace/the-brief-case-for-peters-influence-on-marks-gospel-bible-insert.html.

2. "Word Counts: How Many Times Does a Word Appear in the Bible?," Christian Bible Reference, accessed September 17, 2021, https://www.christianbiblereference.org/faq_WordCount.htm.

3. Blue Letter Bible, s.v. "*arneomai*," accessed July 6, 2021, https://www.blueletterbible.org/lexicon/g720/kjv/tr/0-1/.

4. Catherine Booth, quoted in Robert W. Mitchell, *The Awakening Word* (Bloomington, IN: AuthorHouse, 2011), 164.

CHAPTER 10

1. Thom S. Rainer, "Five Types of Church Members Who Will Not Return After the Quarantine," Church Answers, August 9, 2020, https://churchanswers.com/blog/five-types-of-church-members-who-will-not-return-after-the-quarantine/.

2. David Kinnaman and Gabe Lyons, *unChristian: What a New Generation Really Thinks About Christianity...and Why It Matters* (Grand Rapids, MI: Baker Books, 2007), 82.

3. Winkie Pratney, *Youth Aflame!* (Lindale, TX: Ministry of Helps, 1970), 190.

4. Charles Haddon Spurgeon, "A Sharp Knife for the Vine Branches," sermon, Metropolitan Tabernacle, October 6, 1867, The Spurgeon Center, https://www.spurgeon.org/resource-library/sermons/a-sharp-knife-for-the-vine-branches/#flipbook/.

5. John Wesley, writing to Alexander Mather, quoted in Luke Tyerman, *The Life and Times of the Rev. John Wesley, M.A.: Founder of the Methodists, Vol. III* (London: Hodder & Stoughton, 1870), 632.

CHAPTER 11

1. Blue Letter Bible, s.v. "*kēphas*," accessed July 6, 2021, https://www.blueletterbible.org/lexicon/g2786/kjv/tr/0-1/; Blue Letter Bible, s.v. "*petros*," accessed July 6, 2021, https://www.blueletterbible.org/lexicon/g4074/kjv/tr/0-1/.

2. Henry Blackaby, *Experiencing God: Knowing and Doing the Will of God* (Nashville, TN: B&H Publishers, 2008), 48.

CHAPTER 12

1. "Jacob's Well," See the Holy Land, accessed September 20, 2021, https://www.seetheholyland.net/jacobs-well/.
2. Blue Letter Bible, s.v. *"anexichniastos,"* accessed July 6, 2021, https://www.blueletterbible.org/lexicon/g421/kjv/tr/0-1/.
3. Warren W. Wiersbe, comp., *The Best of A. W. Tozer* (Chicago: Moody Press, 1975), 29.
4. God's recipe for the anointing oil called for a hin of olive oil, and a hin is the equivalent of about one and a half US gallons. See *Merriam-Webster*, s.v. "hin," accessed September 20, 2021, https://www.merriam-webster.com/dictionary/hin.
5. John Stott, *Acts: Seeing the Spirit at Work* (Madison, WI: InterVarsity Press, 2020), 10.
6. Charles H. Spurgeon, *Lectures to My Students* (Grand Rapids, MI: Zondervan, 1954), 195.
7. Dietrich Bonhoeffer, *The Cost of Discipleship* (New York: Touchstone, 1959), 99.
8. Corrie ten Boom with Jamie Buckingham, *Tramp for the Lord* (Fort Washington, PA: CLC Publications, 2011), 63.

About the Author

J. LEE GRADY served for years as a Christian journalist before he became a full-time traveling minister. He worked at *Charisma* magazine from 1992–2010 and served as editor for eleven of those years. In 2000 he launched The Mordecai Project—an international humanitarian organization dedicated to helping women and girls who suffer from various forms of abuse and oppression. Today The Mordecai Project sponsors projects in Latin America, Africa, and Asia to bring the healing of Jesus Christ to those suffering from gender-based violence and discrimination. Grady's missionary work has taken him to thirty-six countries. Find out more at themordecaiproject.org.

Grady's previous books include *10 Lies the Church Tells Women*, *The Truth Sets Women Free*, *10 Lies Men Believe*, *Fearless Daughters of the Bible*, *The Holy Spirit Is Not for Sale*, and *Set My Heart on Fire*—a Bible study about the Holy Spirit. He also writes a weekly column, "Fire in My Bones," which is read by thousands of subscribers to *Charisma*. You can access it for free at fireinmybones.com.

Since 2010 Grady has had a special mandate to disciple and mentor young adults and emerging ministry leaders. He does this through regional Bold Venture retreats for both men and women as well as through individual mentoring. This book,

Follow Me, is a direct outgrowth of his discipleship ministry. You can learn more about Grady at leegrady.com.

If you'd like more information about The Mordecai Project or any of Grady's ministries, email themordecaiproject@gmail.com or write to:

The Mordecai Project / Bold Venture Ministries
PO Box 2781
LaGrange, GA 30241

Read all these inspirational books by J. Lee Grady:

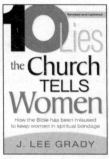  

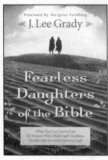  

Dear reader,

I'm so glad you read my book. God is calling you to follow Him on a remarkable journey of building His kingdom and making disciples.

Now that you've read *Follow Me*, be sure to read my companion book, *Let's Go Deeper*. This collection of thirty short lessons on the basics of the Christian faith is the perfect tool to help you disciple another person—whether in a one-on-one setting or in a small group. Or you can study it yourself to grow spiritually—and go deeper with Jesus!

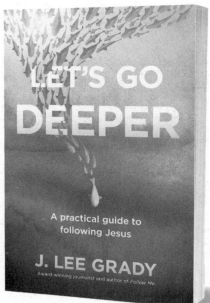

LET'S GO DEEPER

A practical guide to following Jesus

J. LEE GRADY
Award-winning journalist and author of *Follow Me*

Releasing spring 2022